CROCKERY FAVORITES

HEARTLAND COOKING

CROCKERY FAVORITES

FRANCES TOWNER GIEDT

PHOTOGRAPHS BY

Eleanor Thompson

The Reader's Digest Association, Inc.
Pleasantville, New York/Montreal

A Reader's Digest Book

CONCEIVED AND PRODUCED BY
Miller & O'Shea, Inc.

DESIGNED BY
Lynette Cortez Design

The acknowledgments that appear on page 5 are hereby made a part of this copyright page.

Library of Congress Cataloging in Publication Data
Giedt, Frances Towner.
      Crockery favorites /   by Frances Towner Giedt : photographs by
Eleanor Thompson.
      p.   cm. — (Heartland cooking)
      Includes index.
      ISBN 0-89577-853-X
      1. Electric cookery, Slow.   2. Casserole cookery.   I. Title.
II. Series.
TX827.G54 1996
641.5'884— dc20   95- 44745

Printed in the United States of America
Third Printing, August 1997

DEDICATED
WITH LOVE
to my sons, the joys of my life
Brian and Kevin

ACKNOWLEDGMENTS

A COOKBOOK LIKE THIS IS MUCH LIKE THE RECIPES IT CONTAINS, THE RESULT OF MANY INGREDIENTS, slowly simmered. What began as an idea became a complex project involving many people—their help coming in a variety of ways that to acknowledge each and every one's contribution would be an impossible task. Some standouts:

First, a very special word of thanks to my friend Ellie Thompson, the photographer for this book. Also thanks to Karen J.M. Tack, the talented food stylist who prepared the dishes for photography; to Deborah Slocomb, our prop stylist; and to Chris Hobson, a very capable photo assistant.

As always, my thanks and appreciation to Coleen O'Shea and Angela Miller for their guidance and support, to Kathy Knapp for her skillful copy editing, and to Lynette Cortez for her appealing design of this book.

My heartfelt gratitude also to the shops and stores that loaned us the beautiful dishes for the photography of the recipes: Abbey Road Antique Market, Jenks, OK; Anthropology, Westport, CT; The Complete Kitchen, Darien, CT; Dieringer's Arts & Antiques, West Redding, CT; Eddie Bauer Home Design; The Forgotten Garden, Wilton, CT; Francis Hill Antiques, Wilton, CT; L.C.R., Westport, CT; Pier 1 Imports; Pottery Barn; Rebecca's Memories, Jenks, OK; Ridgefield Antique Center, Ridgefield, CT; Rival Manufacturing Company, Kansas City, MO; Simon-Pearce, Westport, CT; Villeroy & Boch; Wayside Exchange & Antiques, Wilton, CT; and Williams-Sonoma. Ironstone stew tureen shown on the cover, courtesy of Dieringer's Arts & Antiques, West Redding, CT.

I also must thank my personal circle of cheerleaders and tasters—my husband and best friend, David; my sons and their wives, Brian and Jackie and Kevin and Kim; and last, my dear friend and hostess while we were photographing this book, Parvine Latimore.

C O N T

E N T S

ICOME FROM A FAIRLY TYPICAL HEARTLAND FAMILY—THE YOUNGEST OF THREE CHILDREN born to a middle-class, middle-America family. Typical of many Heartland families, both of my parents grew up on farms where most of the food for the family table was homegrown. My grandparents tended large vegetable gardens; kept cows for meat, milk, and freshly churned butter; raised pigs for bacon, sausage, and hams; and grew chickens for fresh eggs and fried chicken dinners. At every meal the table was laden with fresh, simply prepared food.

My parents followed this tradition, and as a child I can remember playing hide-and-seek in my father's cornfield and being chased out of my mother's hen house by the resident rooster.

Also typical of the Heartland, my mother's kitchen was the center of family activity. It was the room that

everyone gravitated to and nobody wanted to leave. It was the setting for the dinners that were regular Sunday night events, a weekly gathering of the "clan" that included spouses and grandchildren as each of us married and

INTRO

started a family. Most often these family dinners centered on a pot of stew, soup, pot roast, or other slow-cooking dish that simmered for most of the day at the back of my mother's stove. Since the cooking was done on top of the stove, the dish needed careful watching and frequent addition of liquids.

Happily, today we can get the same wonderful, intensely complex flavors of prolonged cooking without all that fuss in a crockery slow-cooker. But unlike the stovetop dish that needed constant attention, once the crockery slow-cooker is started, you needn't—in fact shouldn't—peek to check on the cooking except when adding ingredients or stirring the food as instructed in these recipes.

With few exceptions, ingredients that can be cooked on top of the stove can be cooked in a slow-cooker. However, some ingredients are best added near the end of the cooking time. The most significant are dairy products, such as milk, cream, sour cream, and cheese; these ingredients tend to separate when cooked for hours.

Slow-cooking is also not recommended for pasta, which will be overcooked by the long cooking time and fall apart. Cook pasta on top of the stove and add it to the slow-cooker near the end of the cooking time.

COOKING ON LOW HEAT

A crockery slow-cooker is designed to cook at a very low temperature, between 200°F and 210°F, or just below the boiling point. Since the liquids do not boil, there is virtually no evaporation. This is why broths in slow-cookers can be bland or "watery" compared to broths

cooked on top of the stove. To compensate, my recipes call for a variety of herbs and spices that combine with the natural moisture of the vegetables, meats, or poultry in each dish to produce incredibly delicious results. If the list of ingredients seems long or complicated, don't despair. The dishes can be assembled quickly, allowing a

speedy getaway in the morning. Or, if your slow-cooker has a removable insert, you can combine the ingredients in the insert in advance, then cover and refrigerate. The next morning, place the insert back in the electric unit to begin the cooking.

Cooking on the LOW setting is truly a "start and forget it" type of cooking. You can even use a household electric timer to start the slow-cooker in your absence. The assem-

bled dish, however, should be thoroughly chilled first and should not stand for more than one hour before the slow-cooker turns on. Don't use the timer for turning the slow-cooker off—it's not wise to let cooked food sit for several hours before being eaten.

COOKING ON HIGH HEAT In addition to the LOW setting, slow-cookers offer a HIGH setting. If your slow-cooker offers more than two settings, consult your manufacturer's instruction manual to determine which temperature levels correspond to LOW and HIGH. When set on HIGH, the unit is cooking at 300°F to 325°F. At this temperature the slow-cooker becomes more like a soup kettle used on top of the stove since the liquids will boil and there will be some moisture loss. When cooking on the HIGH setting, don't leave the slow-cooker unattended for more than the first half of the cooking time since foods can burn and stick if they cook dry. It's also a good idea to stir the food once during the last hour of cooking for some of the recipes on HIGH to prevent the food from sticking. Most of my recipes give directions for both LOW and HIGH settings. When a recipe works well only on either LOW or HIGH, the "cooking time" line specifies only that setting.

DON'T PEEK! When cooking on either LOW or HIGH, there's no need to keep removing the lid to look at the food. Every time you take the lid off, the pot loses the steam that helps the food cook from the top. Once the lid is removed, it takes 15 to 20 minutes to regain the lost steam and temperature. So leave the lid on until the recipe tells you to add last-minute ingredients, to make a sauce, or to stir the food.

REMOVE LEFTOVERS PROMPTLY For food safety, remove any leftover food from your crockery slow-cooker as soon as possible, refrigerating or freezing the leftovers in proper storage containers. Plan on using any refrigerated leftovers within a day or two and frozen leftovers within two months.

TYPES OF CROCKERY SLOW-COOKERS Slow-cookers range in size from 1 to 6 quarts. I developed most of the recipes in this book to fit a 3 ½-quart or a 5-quart slow-cooker, the two most popular sizes. Recipes for a 5-quart or larger slow-cooker give instructions for using the 3½-quart size when appropriate.

The original electric slow-cooker was designed with heating coils embedded in a metal sheath that surrounds the ceramic container for the food. This type of slow-cooker has the continuous slow-cooking needed for the recipes in this book, and it is the type of slow-cooker in which the recipes were tested. In some models, the ceramic container is removable for easy cleaning. Like most small kitchen appliances, the slow-cook-

er plugs into any standard household electrical outlet.

Another type of slow-cooker has the heating coil below the ceramic container. This slow-cooker has a dial indicating temperatures in degrees and a heating element that cycles on and off. Consult your manufacturer's instruction manual guidelines for using these recipes with your slow-cooker.

HIGH-ALTITUDE SLOW-COOKING If you live in a high-altitude area and you already extend cooking times for conventional stovetop cooking, your slow-cooker times will also be correspondingly longer than those my recipes specify. The first time you use a recipe, note the change in the cooking time for future use.

A VARIETY OF RECIPES The thirteen states of America's Heartland—Kansas, Illinois, Indiana, Iowa, Michigan, Minnesota, Missouri, Nebraska, North Dakota, Ohio, Oklahoma, South Dakota, and Wisconsin—are richly diverse in their ethnic roots. This is strongly reflected in the food of the region. In addition to the recipes brought by the English migrating to the Midwest from New England, you'll find Midwestern recipes that range from Hungarian in heritage to Italian in origin. There are vast areas populated by people of Russian-German extraction and large pockets of first-generation Americans from Poland, Finland, Norway, and Sweden. Much of the food of Oklahoma and Missouri has a Southern influence. With the influx of immigrants from Mexico, and more recently from Vietnam, such ingredients as chile peppers, cilantro, and lemon grass have become commonplace in many Heartland supermarkets.

In this book I offer a collection of slow-cooker recipes that use the indigenous foods of the region and truly reflect the way Midwesterners cook today. Some of these recipes are updated versions of my mother's or other family members' recipes, adapted for the slow-cooker. Others were developed in my kitchen and have passed the critical taste-testing of my family and friends.

Here you'll find recipes for soups and stews to warm you on a cold winter day. Poultry is a mainstay of Midwestern cooks. In the poultry and game section, there are mouth-watering recipes that bring out the robust flavor of chicken, duck, turkey, pheasant, rabbit, and game hen. The meats section showcases the variety of meats found in the Midwest, plenty of recipes for beef, pork, veal, and lamb with a depth of flavor produced only through hours of slow-cooking at a low heat. A crockery slow-cooker is particularly well suited to the foods that are the

center of a vegetarian diet. In the vegetarian dishes section you'll find delicious recipes based on dried beans and slow-cooked vegetables. At the back of the book you'll find a few recipes for delightfully delicious desserts to prove that your crockery slow-cooker can produce the most luscious food you've ever cooked. So dig your sixties model out of the closet or invest in a newer slow-cooker and start crockery cooking!

NUTRITIONAL INFORMATION For these recipes the nutritional analysis uses the most current data from "The Food Processor," Version 6.02, by ESHA Research, and the United States Department of Agriculture. Nutritional information is given for calories; grams of protein, total fat and saturated fat, carbohydrates, and dietary fiber; and milligrams of sodium and cholesterol. The nutritional analysis does not include optional ingredients or those for which no specific amount is stated.

METRIC CONVERSION CHART

LIQUID AND DRY MEASURE EQUIVALENTS

Customary	Metric
¼ teaspoon	1.25 milliliters
½ teaspoon	2.5 milliliters
1 teaspoon	5 milliliters
1 tablespoon	15 milliliters
1 fluid ounce	30 milliliters
¼ cup	60 milliliters
⅓ cup	80 milliliters
½ cup	120 milliliters
1 cup	240 milliliters
1 pint (2 cups)	480 milliliters
1 quart (4 cups; 32 ounces)	960 milliliters (.35 liter)
1 gallon (4 quarts)	3.84 liters
1 ounce (by weight)	28.35 grams
¼ pound (4 ounces)	114 grams
1 pound (16 ounces)	454 grams
2.2 pounds	1 kilogram (1,000 grams)

TEMPERATURE EQUIVALENTS

Description	°Fahrenheit	°Celsius
Cool	200	90
Very slow	250	120
Slow	300–325	150–160
Moderately slow	325–350	160–180
Moderate	350–375	180–190
Moderately hot	375–400	190–200
Hot	400–450	200–230
Very hot	450–500	230–260

COOKING AND BAKING EQUIVALENTS

Bakeware	Customary	Metric
Round Pan	8 x 1½ inches	20 x 4 cm
	9 x 1½ inches	23 x 4 cm
	10 x 1½ inches	25 x 4 cm
Square Pan	8 x 8 x 2 inches	20 x 20 x 5 cm
	9 x 9 x 2 inches	23 x 23 x 5 cm
Baking Dishes	7 x 11 x 1½ inches	18 x 28 x 4 cm
	7½ x 12 x 2 inches	19 x 30 x 5 cm
	9 x 13 x 2 inches	23 x 33 x 5 cm
Loaf Pan	4½ x 8½ x 2½ inches	11 x 21 x 6 cm
	5 x 9 x 3 inches	13 x 23 x 8 cm
Muffin Cups	2½ x 1¼ inches	6 x 3 cm
	3 x 1½ inches	8 x 4 cm
Casseroles and Saucepans	1 quart	1 L
	1½ quart	1.5 L
	2 quart	2 L
	2½ quart	2.5 L
	3 quart	3 L
	4 quart	4 L

SOUPS AND STEWS

THERE'S NOTHING MORE COMFORTING or inviting on a cold wintery night as a bowl of soup or a plate of stew. Complete by themselves, they require only a crisp salad, a warm loaf of crusty bread, and a simple dessert to make a meal special enough for company.

Ironically, a sizable piece of meat takes less time to cook in a crockery slow-cooker than a whole carrot or potato. Because vegetables cook so slowly, it's important to cut them in the sizes specified in the recipes and to layer the ingredients as directed. The appearance and texture of the soup or stew will be determined by how finely or coarsely the vegetables are cut. Chopped means pieces cut at about ¼-inch intervals; coarsely chopped means ½-inch pieces or pieces cut haphazardly. Some recipes will instruct you to stir the dish; others will not. For best results, follow the recipe instructions.

If you often make soup and you're concerned about your salt intake, you'll need to make your own stocks (it's easy in a slow-cooker—check the Index for specific recipes) and freeze them in measured quantities to use in these recipes. If you prefer to use canned broth or a bouillon cube, just be sure it's labeled *low-sodium* to comply with the sodium levels calculated for these recipes.

BEEF AND WINTER VEGETABLE SOUP

MAKES 4 SERVINGS

In earlier times this recipe would have been called Root Cellar Soup, for it uses many of the root vegetables that were stored beneath Heartland farmhouses.

It's a rich, wintery soup, sure to fortify after a day of outdoor activities. Some crusty bread, a wedge of cheese, and some crisp winter pears make for a soul-satisfying meal.

1 pound top round, well trimmed and cut into 1-inch cubes
  Salt, optional, and freshly ground black pepper to taste
1 tablespoon olive oil
2 medium yellow onions, chopped (2 cups)
2 large garlic cloves, chopped
2 medium parsnips, peeled and cut into 1-inch pieces (2 cups)
2 medium russet potatoes, scrubbed and cut into 1-inch pieces (2 cups)
2 medium carrots, peeled and cut into 1-inch pieces (1½ cups)

2 medium celery ribs, chopped (1 cup)
½ pound fresh button mushrooms, thickly sliced (2½ cups)
1 tablespoon chopped fresh thyme leaves or 1 teaspoon dried, crumbled
1 large bay leaf
1 quart beef stock (page 82) or canned low-sodium broth
¼ cup dry red wine
1 10-ounce package frozen baby lima beans
¼ cup sour cream
2 slices bacon, cooked crisp and crumbled

**PREP TIME:
25 MIN**

**COOK TIME:
8-10 HR ON LOW +
15 MIN ON HIGH
OR 4¼-5¼ HR
ON HIGH**

1. Season beef with salt and pepper. In a large skillet, brown beef in oil over medium-high heat for 5 minutes, turning beef to brown all sides.

2. Transfer beef to a 3½-quart or larger crockery slow-cooker. Top with onions and garlic. Add in layers the parsnips, potatoes, carrots, and celery. Scatter mushrooms and thyme over the top. Add the bay leaf. Pour in stock and wine. Do not stir. Cover and cook on LOW for 8 to 10 hours or on HIGH for 4 to 5 hours.

3. If cooking on LOW, change setting to HIGH. Stir in lima beans. Cover and cook until beans are just tender, about 15 minutes. Discard bay leaf. Ladle into wide, shallow soup bowls. Dollop sour cream onto each serving and sprinkle with bacon.

Per serving: 513 calories, 42 g protein, 14 g total fat (4.9 g saturated), 52 g carbohydrates, 247 mg sodium, 80 mg cholesterol, 12 g dietary fiber

CABBAGE AND PORK SOUP

MAKES 4 SERVINGS

Another great cold-weather meal that will chase away the winter blues. Serve with hot corn bread. For dessert, top baked apples or pears with a dollop of vanilla ice cream or frozen yogurt.

1 pound boneless pork loin, trimmed of fat and cut into 1-inch cubes

1 tablespoon olive oil

3 slices bacon, cut into 1-inch pieces and blanched in boiling water

1 large yellow onion, cut in half and thinly sliced (2 cups)

2 large garlic cloves, minced

2 medium russet potatoes, scrubbed and cut into 1-inch pieces (2 cups)

2 medium carrots, peeled and cut into ½-inch pieces (1½ cups)

6 cups chicken stock (page 53) or canned low-sodium broth

½ pound green cabbage, trimmed, cored, quartered, and thinly sliced (2 cups)

3 tablespoons minced red onion for garnish

PREP TIME: 20 MIN

COOK TIME: 7½–9½ HR ON LOW + 15 MIN ON HIGH OR 4¼–5¼ HR ON HIGH

1. In a large skillet, brown pork pieces in oil over medium-high heat for 5 minutes.

2. Using a slotted spoon, transfer pork to a 3½-quart or larger crockery slow-cooker. Cover with blanched bacon, yellow onion, and garlic. Top with potatoes, then carrots. Add stock. Do not stir. Cover and cook on LOW for 7½ to 9½ hours or on HIGH for 4 to 5 hours.

3. If cooking on LOW, change setting to HIGH. Add cabbage, cover, and cook until cabbage is tender to bite, about 15 minutes. Ladle into wide, shallow soup bowls. Garnish with red onion.

Per serving: 413 calories, 36 g protein, 18 g total fat (5.5 g saturated), 25 g carbohydrates, 288 mg sodium, 75 mg cholesterol, 4 g dietary fiber

FRESH CHILE PEPPERS

Be careful when working with fresh chile peppers. The source of heat that inflames your mouth (an odorless substance called *capsaicin* that's concentrated in the veins and seeds of the chile) can do the same thing to your hands, eyes, and nose. Always wear rubber gloves and immediately after working with chiles, wash your hands with soap and hot water.

When shopping, choose chile peppers that are shiny and firm, have no deep creases or bends, and are heavy for their size. Chiles are best kept loose in the vegetable bin of the refrigerator and will stay fresh for up to one week.

Fresh chile peppers are generally available throughout the United States, although in more remote areas you may need to track down a Hispanic or Latin grocery store. Listed from the mildest to the hottest, the peppers called for in these recipes are:

Anaheim: One of the most common and readily available, this chile is very mild and pale green (occasionally red), tapered, about 4 to 6 inches long, and 2 inches around.

Poblano: A medium-hot dark green chile, 4 to 5 inches long and 3 to 4 inches around.

Jalapeño: Dark green or red, the jalapeño is the best known and most widely used hot chile in the United States, estimated to be available in more than 90 percent of today's supermarkets. It measures 1½ to 3 inches in length and 1 inch across the stem end, tapering to a rounded end.

Habañero: The hottest chile, the habañero is very small and lantern-shaped, like a miniature bell pepper or pimiento. It may be green, yellow, or orange.

CINCINNATI CHILI FIVE WAYS

MAKES 6 SERVINGS

Created in 1922 by John Kiradjieff, the founder of the Empress Chili Parlor, Cincinnati Chili is full of the aromatic spices of his Greek homeland. The chili is traditionally served over hot spaghetti, but no one knows for sure the exact blend of spices that he used. Today there are scores of chili parlors in the Queen City, each serving a slightly different version. The recipes are such a closely guarded secret that the actual mixing of the spices takes place behind closed doors away from the kitchen. My version looks complicated, but it goes together quite easily.

Cincinnati Chili can be ordered "One Way" (plain), "Two Ways" (over spaghetti), "Three Ways" (over spaghetti with grated Cheddar cheese on top), "Four Ways" (over spaghetti with grated cheese and chopped onions), and "Five Ways" (over spaghetti with grated cheese, chopped onions, and dark red kidney beans). A bowl of oyster crackers is served alongside.

1½ pounds ground beef round
2 medium yellow onions, chopped (2 cups)
1 medium celery rib, chopped (½ cup)
4 large garlic cloves, minced
2 tablespoons chili powder
1 tablespoon paprika
½ tablespoon chopped fresh basil leaves or ½ teaspoon dried, crumbled
½ tablespoon chopped fresh oregano leaves or ½ teaspoon dried, crumbled
½ tablespoon chopped fresh thyme leaves or ½ teaspoon dried, crumbled
1 teaspoon ground cinnamon
½ teaspoon cayenne pepper
½ teaspoon ground cumin
½ teaspoon crushed red pepper

¼ teaspoon ground allspice
Salt, optional, and freshly ground black pepper to taste
1 28-ounce can peeled tomatoes in purée undrained
1 8-ounce can tomato sauce
½ cup water
1 pound dried thin spaghetti, broken in half

T O P P I N G S

¾ cup grated sharp Cheddar cheese (3 ounces)
1 medium yellow onion, chopped (1 cup)
1 15½-ounce can dark red kidney beans, heated and drained

Oyster crackers

PREP TIME:
25 MIN

COOK TIME:
7–9 HR ON LOW
OR 3½–4½ HR
ON HIGH

1. In a large skillet, brown ground beef, onions, celery, and garlic over medium-high heat until the beef is browned and the onions are limp, about 5 minutes. Drain off all fat.
2. Transfer meat mixture to a 3½-quart or larger crockery slow-cooker and combine with remaining ingredients except spaghetti and Toppings. Stir to mix well. Cover and cook on LOW for 7 to 9 hours or on HIGH for 3½ to 4½ hours. Stir once during the last hour if cooking on HIGH.
3. About 30 minutes before serving, cook spaghetti according to package directions. Drain and keep warm.
4. Stir the chili. Serve in wide, shallow soup bowls, ladled over a serving of hot spaghetti. Garnish with cheese, onion, and beans. Serve with oyster crackers on the side.

Per serving: 698 calories, 42 g protein, 21 g total fat (8.7 g saturated), 86 g carbohydrates, 832 mg sodium, 88 mg cholesterol, 16 g dietary fiber

FIVE-ALARM CHILI

MAKES 6 SERVINGS

Some like it hot! Serve this blazing good chili with a spicy yogurt topping, grated Wisconsin Colby cheese, and lots of iced tea or cold beer to put out the fire.

Developed in 1885 by Joseph Steinwald, the son of a cheese-maker in the small town of Colby, Wisconsin, Colby cheese is a mild-flavored fresh cheese with a softer texture than an aged Cheddar. It melts readily into the hot chili. If you prefer a sharp cheese, feel free to substitute.

2   pounds ground beef round
1   large yellow onion, chopped (1½ cups)
2   large garlic cloves, minced
1   tablespoon olive oil
1   large red bell pepper, seeded and coarsely chopped (1½ cups)
2   jalapeño chile peppers, seeded and minced
¼   cup chili powder
2   tablespoons chopped fresh oregano or 2 teaspoons dried, crumbled
1   tablespoon ground cumin
2   14½-ounce cans whole tomatoes, undrained and chopped

1½ cups beef stock (page 82) or canned low-sodium broth
1   15½-ounce can pinto beans, rinsed and drained

SPICY TOPPING

1   cup plain yogurt
¼   cup chopped fresh cilantro
½   tablespoon chili powder
½   teaspoon onion powder
¼   teaspoon cayenne pepper

¾   cup grated Colby cheese (3 ounces)

1. In a large skillet, brown beef, onion, and garlic in oil over medium-high heat, stirring constantly, about 5 minutes. Drain off excess oil.

2. Using a slotted spoon, transfer beef mixture to a 3½-quart or larger crockery slow-cooker and combine with remaining ingredients except the Spicy Topping and cheese. Stir to mix well. Cover and cook on LOW for 8 to 10 hours or on HIGH for 4 to 5 hours. Stir once during the last hour if cooking on HIGH.

3. Meanwhile, in a small bowl, combine ingredients for topping. Stir well to blend evenly. Refrigerate until ready to use. Return to room temperature before spooning a dollop onto each serving of chili. Sprinkle with Colby cheese and serve.

PREP TIME:
20 MIN

COOK TIME:
8–10 HR ON LOW
OR 4–5 HR
ON HIGH

Per serving: 505 calories, 40 g protein, 29 g total fat (11.6 g saturated), 23 g carbohydrates, 595 mg sodium, 116 mg cholesterol, 7 g dietary fiber

FRESH CORN AND FISH CHOWDER

MAKES 4 SERVINGS

The Heartland grows more sweet corn than any other part of the country. Most every state has at least one special event to celebrate the bumper crop, complete with parades, competitions, and pageants.

This lovely fish soup is enhanced by farm-fresh corn. To remove the kernels from the cob, hold the cob vertically over a wide, shallow pan. Using a sharp knife, slice straight down to cut under the kernels, letting them fall into the pan. If fresh corn is not in season, you can substitute the same amount of frozen corn kernels to good effect.

1 medium fennel bulb, trimmed and coarsely chopped, reserving feathery fronds (2 cups)
1 large red onion, chopped (1½ cups)
2 large garlic cloves, minced
1 teaspoon chopped fresh rosemary leaves or ¼ teaspoon dried, crumbled
4 small red potatoes, scrubbed and cut into 1-inch pieces (2 cups)
1 28-ounce can Italian plum tomatoes, undrained and chopped

1 quart chicken stock (page 53) or canned low-sodium broth
Freshly ground black pepper to taste
1 pound skinless halibut or swordfish fillets, cut into 1-inch cubes
Corn kernels cut from 4 medium ears (2 cups)

PREP TIME: 20 MIN
COOK TIME: 6–8 HR ON LOW + 15 MIN ON HIGH OR 3¼–4¼ HR ON HIGH

1. In a 3½-quart or larger crockery slow-cooker, combine fennel, onion, garlic, and rosemary. Top with potatoes, tomatoes, and stock. Sprinkle generously with pepper. Do not stir. Cover and cook on LOW for 6 to 8 hours or on HIGH for 3 to 4 hours.

2. If cooking on LOW, change setting to HIGH. Stir in halibut and corn. Continue to cook, covered, for 15 minutes, until fish flakes easily with a fork and corn kernels are just tender.

3. To serve, ladle chowder into wide, shallow soup bowls. Chop reserved fennel fronds and sprinkle over each serving.

Per serving: 363 calories, 36 g protein, 6 g total fat (1.0 g saturated), 46 g carbohydrates, 505 mg sodium, 36 mg cholesterol, 8 g dietary fiber

GREEN BEAN AND STEAK SOUP

MAKES 6 SERVINGS

My mother always grew green beans in her garden. A lot ended up canned for the winter months, but each week during the summer several pounds would be cooked the old-fashioned way, long-simmered to tenderness for that night's supper.

In this satisfying soup the vibrant color of fresh green beans is sacrificed for extra depth of flavor. Accompany the soup with warm crusty bread and a crisp salad.

If using a 3½- or 4-quart slow-cooker, prepare half of the recipe.

4 slices bacon, cut into ½-inch pieces	3 large garlic cloves, minced
2 pounds lean boneless beef sirloin, trimmed of fat and cut into 1½-inch pieces	6 cups beef stock (page 82) or canned low-sodium broth
1 pound green beans, trimmed and cut into 1-inch lengths	1 large bay leaf
2 medium yellow onions, chopped (2 cups)	½ teaspoon dried dill weed
3 medium plum tomatoes, chopped (1 cup)	2 cups hot cooked rice
2 medium celery ribs, thinly sliced (1 cup)	Chopped fresh flat-leaf parsley for garnish

PREP TIME: 25 MIN

COOK TIME: 8–10 HR ON LOW OR 4–5 HR ON HIGH

1. In a large skillet over medium heat, cook bacon until lightly browned. Using a slotted spoon, transfer bacon to a 5-quart or larger crockery slow-cooker. Discard all but 1 tablespoon of the drippings. Add steak to skillet and brown on all sides, about 10 minutes.

2. Transfer steak to slow-cooker and mix with bacon. Top with green beans, onions, tomatoes, celery, and garlic. Add stock, bay leaf, and dill. Do not stir. Cover and cook on LOW for 8 to 10 hours or on HIGH for 4 to 5 hours.

3. To serve, stir soup and ladle into wide, shallow soup bowls. Discard bay leaf. Spoon ⅓ cup cooked rice into the middle of each serving. Sprinkle with parsley and serve.

Per serving: 453 calories, 45 g protein, 16 g total fat (5.9 g saturated), 31 g carbohydrates, 249 mg sodium, 108 mg cholesterol, 4 g dietary fiber

HEARTLAND CLAM AND SHRIMP CHOWDER

MAKES 6 SERVINGS

Even landlubbers love a bowl of steamy chowder loaded with clams. Small shrimp add an extra dimension to this rich soup. If you're tailgating, take this soup along in a preheated thermos to serve with a crisp green salad, some seasonal fresh fruit, and crusty bread for a simple but satisfying lunch. ▶

HEARTLAND CLAM AND SHRIMP CHOWDER *(see previous page for photo and notes)*

1 large yellow onion, chopped
(1½ cups)

1 large leek with 1 inch pale-green top,
well rinsed and chopped (1⅓ cups)

2 large garlic cloves, minced

2 medium carrots, peeled and thinly
sliced (1½ cups)

2 medium celery ribs, thinly sliced
(1 cup)

2 medium thin-skinned potatoes, scrubbed
and cut into 1-inch pieces (2 cups)

1 8-ounce bottle clam juice

2 cups chicken stock (page 53)
or canned low-sodium broth

2 teaspoons fresh thyme leaves
or ½ teaspoon dried, crumbled

2 cups half-and-half

2 tablespoons butter, at room temperature,
optional

2 tablespoons unbleached all-purpose
flour, optional

2 10-ounce cans baby clams, drained

1 pound small peeled cooked shrimp

3 slices bacon, cooked crisp and
crumbled

Paprika for sprinkling

PREP TIME: 20 MIN

COOK TIME: 6–8 HR ON LOW + 30 MIN ON HIGH OR 3½–4½ HR ON HIGH

1. In a 3½-quart or larger crockery slow-cooker, layer onion, leek, garlic, carrots, celery, and potatoes. Pour in clam juice, stock, and thyme. Do not stir. Cover and cook on LOW for 6 to 8 hours or on HIGH for 3 to 4 hours.

2. If cooking on LOW, change setting to HIGH. Stir in half-and-half. If a thicker chowder is desired, mix together butter and flour. Stir into chowder. Add clams, shrimp, and bacon. Cook, uncovered, stirring occasionally, until chowder is thickened and steaming, about 30 minutes.

3. Ladle into wide, shallow soup bowls and sprinkle with paprika.

Per serving: 400 calories, 35 g protein, 17 g total fat (9.2 g saturated), 26 g carbohydrates, 584 mg sodium, 222 mg cholesterol, 3 g dietary fiber

LIMA BEAN
AND HAM CHOWDER

MAKES 6 SERVINGS

This chowder is the kind of hearty soup that fortifies after a day of outdoor activity. If you want a thinner soup, add more chicken broth. Serve the chowder with some freshly made muffins, a bunch of chilled grapes, and a wedge of cheese.

1 pound dried baby lima beans, rinsed and picked over (2 cups)

6 cups water

2 cups diced lean smoked fully cooked ham

2 large yellow onions, chopped (3 cups)

2 large garlic cloves, minced

2 medium celery ribs with leaves, chopped (1½ cups)

3 small red potatoes, scrubbed and diced (1 cup)

2 medium tomatoes, chopped (2 cups)

1 large bay leaf

1 tablespoon chopped fresh oregano leaves or 1 teaspoon dried, crumbled

1 tablespoon chopped fresh thyme leaves or 1 teaspoon dried, crumbled

½ tablespoon chopped fresh basil leaves or ½ teaspoon dried, crumbled

¼ teaspoon crushed red pepper

5 cups chicken stock (page 53) or canned low-sodium broth

2 green onions, thinly sliced, for garnish

1. In a 3½-quart or larger crockery slow-cooker, soak beans in water overnight or for at least 6 hours. Or put beans and water in a large pot and bring to a boil on top of the stove. Boil for 2 minutes, turn off heat, and let stand 1 hour. Drain beans and place in slow-cooker.
2. Layer remaining ingredients except green onions in slow-cooker. Do not stir. Cover and cook on LOW for 7 to 9 hours or on HIGH for 4½ to 5½ hours. Discard bay leaf.
3. If a thicker chowder is desired, remove 2 cups of the soup and slightly mash the beans. Return to the slow-cooker and stir. Ladle into soup bowls. Sprinkle with sliced green onions.

PREP TIME: 25 MIN + AT LEAST 1¼ HR FOR SOAKING BEANS

COOK TIME: 7–9 HR ON LOW OR 4½–5½ HR ON HIGH

Per serving: 381 calories, 28 g protein, 4 g total fat (1.0 g saturated), 61 g carbohydrates, 566 mg sodium, 19 mg cholesterol, 16 g dietary fiber

MIXED BEAN AND CHICKEN SOUP

MAKES 6 SERVINGS

You can buy prepackaged mixed dried beans with instructions for making bean soup. But if you're like me, you probably already have several kinds of beans in your pantry. The amounts given for the beans can be changed according to what you have on hand. You can also substitute other legumes such as split peas or lentils as long as you end up with 2 cups of mixed beans.

1 cup dried white beans, rinsed and picked over
½ cup dried red kidney beans, rinsed and picked over
¼ cup dried baby lima beans, rinsed and picked over
2 tablespoons dried black turtle beans, rinsed and picked over
2 tablespoons dried black-eyed peas, rinsed and picked over
6 cups water
1 pound boneless, skinless chicken breasts, cut into 1-inch cubes
1 medium yellow onion, coarsely chopped (1 cup)

1 medium celery rib, coarsely chopped (½ cup)
2 large garlic cloves, minced
6 cups chicken stock (page 53) or canned low-sodium broth
¼ cup dry white wine
½ tablespoon chopped fresh thyme leaves or ½ teaspoon dried, crumbled
⅛ teaspoon cayenne pepper
1 large bay leaf
   Salt, optional, and freshly ground black pepper to taste
   Chopped fresh flat-leaf parsley for garnish
   Balsamic vinegar or lemon wedges for garnish

**PREP TIME:
25 MIN + AT
LEAST 1¼ HR FOR
SOAKING BEANS**

**COOK TIME:
8–10 HR ON LOW
OR 4–5 HR
ON HIGH**

1. In a 3½-quart or larger crockery slow-cooker, soak beans and black-eyed peas in water overnight or for at least 6 hours. Or put beans, black-eyed peas, and water in a large pot and bring to a boil on top of the stove. Boil for 2 minutes, turn off heat, and let stand 1 hour. Drain and put beans and black-eyed peas in the slow-cooker.

2. Layer remaining ingredients except salt, pepper, parsley, and vinegar in slow-cooker. Do not stir. Cover and cook on LOW for 8 to 10 hours or on HIGH for 4 to 5 hours. When ready to serve, discard bay leaf. Add salt and pepper.

3. If a thicker soup is desired, using a slotted spoon, remove 1 cup of the beans and slightly mash. Return to the slow-cooker and stir. Ladle into wide, shallow soup bowls. Sprinkle each serving with parsley. Pass a cruet of balsamic vinegar to drizzle or lemon wedges to squeeze into the soup.

Per serving: 363 calories, 37 g protein, 3 g total fat (0.8 g saturated), 45 g carbohydrates, 136 mg sodium, 44 mg cholesterol, 13 g dietary fiber

NAVY BEAN CHOWDER WITH HOT SALSA

MAKES 6 SERVINGS

Michigan grows most of the world's supply of navy beans—a small white legume so named when it became a staple pantry item of the United States Navy in the mid-1800s.

This hearty navy bean soup is just the thing for chilly autumn evenings. You'll love the combination of texture, flavor, and color. The hot salsa garnish adds a zippy fresh flavor.

1 pound dried navy beans (2 cups)

6 cups water

4 slices bacon, cut into 1-inch pieces and blanched in boiling water

3 small red potatoes, scrubbed and cut into eighths

2 medium yellow onions, chopped (2 cups)

2 large garlic cloves, minced

2 large celery ribs, chopped (2 cups)

1 medium red bell pepper, seeded and cut into ½-inch pieces (1 cup)

1 medium yellow bell pepper, seeded and cut into ½-inch pieces (1 cup)

1 medium carrot, peeled and chopped (¾ cup)

1 tablespoon chopped fresh thyme leaves or 1 teaspoon dried, crumbled

5 cups chicken stock (page 53) or canned low-sodium broth

HOT SALSA

1 medium tomato, peeled and coarsely chopped (1 cup)

1 medium Anaheim chile pepper, seeded and coarsely chopped (¼ cup)

1 small jalapeño chile pepper, seeded and coarsely chopped

Juice of 1 medium lime (1 tablespoon)

¼ cup chopped fresh cilantro

1. In a 3½-quart or larger crockery slow-cooker, soak beans in water overnight or for at least 6 hours. Or put beans and water in a large pot and bring to a boil on top of the stove. Boil for 2 minutes, turn off heat, and let stand 1 hour. Drain beans and place in the slow-cooker.

2. Add the remaining ingredients except salsa. Stir to mix well. Cover and cook on LOW for 8 to 10 hours or on HIGH for 4 to 5 hours.

3. To make Hot Salsa: Place all ingredients in a food processor or blender. Chop, using the on/off switch, until mixture is finely minced.

4. If a thicker chowder is desired, using a slotted spoon, remove 1 cup of the beans and slightly mash. Return to the slow-cooker and stir. Ladle into soup bowls, garnishing with a spoonful of salsa in the center.

PREP TIME:
25 MIN + AT
LEAST 1¼ HR FOR
SOAKING BEANS

COOK TIME:
8–10 HR ON LOW
OR 4–5 HR
ON HIGH

Per serving: 411 calories, 24 g protein, 8 g total fat (2.6 g saturated), 63 g carbohydrates, 179 mg sodium, 7 mg cholesterol, 21 g dietary fiber

OLD-FASHIONED CHICKEN SOUP WITH HOMEMADE NOODLES

MAKES 6 SERVINGS

I doubt if my mother ever bought a package of noodles. She considered them so easy to make—and always better than store-bought. I agree!

For a 3½- 4-quart slow-cooker, use 1½ pounds boneless, skinless chicken breasts or thighs instead of bone-in chicken. Substitute 2 cups boiling chicken stock for 2 cups of the boiling water.

1 3-to 3½-pound chicken, cut into 8 pieces
1 large onion, peeled and quartered
1 large carrot, peeled and quartered
3 sprigs fresh flat-leaf parsley
½ tablespoon fresh thyme leaves
   or ½ teaspoon dried, crumbled
½ tablespoon chopped fresh marjoram leaves
   or ½ teaspoon dried, crumbled
¼ teaspoon freshly ground black pepper

1 quart chicken stock (page 53) or canned
   low-sodium broth
   Homemade Noodles (recipe follows)
1 quart boiling water
½ pound fresh button mushrooms, sliced
   (2½ cups)
½ pound fresh spinach, well washed and stems
   removed (6 cups)

1. Rinse chicken and pat dry. Discard neck and giblets or reserve for another use. Put chicken, onion, and carrot in a 5-quart or larger crockery slow-cooker. Sprinkle with parsley, thyme, marjoram, and pepper. Add stock, cover, and cook on LOW for 7 to 8 hours or on HIGH for 2½ to 3 hours.

2. At least 1 hour before the soup is done, make the noodles.

3. Remove chicken from broth and cool for about 10 minutes or until just cool enough to handle. Discard onion, carrot, and parsley. Remove and discard chicken skin and bones. Shred chicken and set aside.

4. If cooking on LOW, change setting to HIGH. Add boiling water, noodles, mushrooms, and spinach. Cook, uncovered, until spinach wilts and noodles are tender, about 5 minutes. Gently stir in reserved chicken. Heat through. Ladle into wide, shallow soup bowls.

PREP TIME:
30 MIN

COOK TIME:
7–8 HR ON LOW +
15 MIN ON HIGH
OR 2³/₄–3¹/₄ HR
ON HIGH

Per serving: 238 calories, 31 g protein, 6 g total fat (1.4 g saturated), 15 g carbohydrates, 352 mg sodium, 112 mg cholesterol, 2 g dietary fiber

HOMEMADE NOODLES

1 large egg
½ teaspoon salt
⅔ cup unbleached all-purpose flour

1. In a bowl, beat together egg and salt using a fork. While stirring, gradually add flour. Using your hands, form the mixture into a ball.

2. On a lightly floured work surface, knead the dough for 30 seconds. Using a rolling pin, roll the dough to form a very thin 10 x 18-inch rectangle. Working from the long side, roll the dough up jelly-roll fashion. Slice across roll into rings about ¼ inch wide.

3. Unroll or shake out the rings to form long noodles. Place noodles on a large baking sheet or kitchen towel. Let rest for 20 to 30 minutes before adding to the soup.

PORK CHILI WITH HOMINY

MAKES 8 SERVINGS

When I was growing up, we frequently had hominy, dried white or yellow corn kernels from which the hull and germ have been removed. My mother would fry canned ready-to-eat hominy to serve as a side dish, but I didn't develop a fondness for it until I was an adult. Now I find myself using it in both its whole form and ground (grits). It adds a unique flavor and textural contrast to this spicy chili.

With the increasing Mexican population in most every Midwestern state, ingredients such as tomatillos, the small vegetable that resembles a green tomato in a parchment paper husk, and cilantro are now commonplace and easily found in most supermarkets. You'll need both for this chili. See page 19 for help in finding the right kind of chile peppers.

If using a 3½- or 4-quart slow-cooker, prepare half of the recipe.

1 pound dried pink beans, rinsed and picked over (2 cups)
6 cups water
1 large red bell pepper
2 medium poblano chile peppers
1 small habañero chile pepper
1 tablespoon chopped fresh oregano leaves or 1 teaspoon dried, crumbled
1 tablespoon chili powder
3 large garlic cloves, minced
1½ teaspoons ground coriander
1 teaspoon ground cumin
½ teaspoon freshly ground black pepper

2 pounds well-trimmed boneless pork shoulder, cut into 1-inch cubes
2 medium yellow onions, chopped (2 cups)
5 medium tomatillos, husked, rinsed, and chopped (1½ cups)
1 28-ounce can Italian plum tomatoes, undrained and coarsely chopped
2 16-ounce cans yellow or white hominy, drained and rinsed
½ cup chopped fresh cilantro
24 tortilla chips
½ cup sour cream

PREP TIME: 35 MIN + AT LEAST 1¼ HR FOR SOAKING BEANS

COOK TIME: 6–8 HR ON LOW + 15 MIN ON HIGH OR 3¼–4¼ HR ON HIGH

1. In a 5-quart or larger crockery slow-cooker, soak beans in water overnight or for at least 6 hours. Or put beans and water in a large pot and bring to a boil on top of the stove. Boil for 2 minutes, turn off heat, and let stand 1 hour. Drain beans and place in the slow-cooker.
2. Meanwhile, roast the bell pepper, poblanos, and habañero under the broiler, turning frequently, until blackened all over. Transfer peppers to a paper bag, close, and let steam for 10 minutes. Peel under running water, removing the stems, seeds, and ribs. Drain or pat dry with paper towels. Finely chop.
3. In a large self-sealing plastic bag, shake oregano, chili powder, garlic, coriander, cumin, and black pepper to combine. Add pork pieces and shake to coat evenly.
4. Combine pork mixture with onions, tomatillos, and chopped chiles. Place in slow-cooker on top of beans. Top with tomatoes. Do not stir. Cover and cook on LOW for 6 to 8 hours or on HIGH for 3 to 4 hours.
5. About 15 minutes before serving, stir in drained hominy. If cooking on LOW, change setting to HIGH. Cook, covered, until hominy is heated through. Stir in cilantro. Spoon chili into bowls. Top each serving with 3 tortilla chips and a dollop of sour cream.

Per serving: 543 calories, 40 g protein, 16 g total fat (5.5 g saturated), 63 g carbohydrates, 470 mg sodium, 89 mg cholesterol, 15 g dietary fiber

TURKEY AND WILD RICE SOUP

MAKES 6 SERVINGS

When I think of comfort food, this soup comes to mind. Make this to enjoy in front of a blazing fire on a blustery day. Wild rice, actually not rice at all but a long-grain marsh grass native to the Great Lakes region of Minnesota, adds a subtle flavor and chewy texture to this soup.

1   cup wild rice, well rinsed and drained
1   tablespoon mild vegetable oil, such as canola
1   large leek, white part only, well rinsed and chopped (1 cup)
1   large yellow onion, chopped (1½ cups)
2   medium celery ribs, coarsely chopped (1 cup)
1½ pounds boneless, skinless turkey breast, cut into 1½-inch cubes
½   tablespoon fresh thyme leaves or ½ teaspoon dried, crumbled

½   tablespoon chopped fresh oregano leaves or ½ teaspoon dried, crumbled
½   teaspoon freshly ground black pepper Salt, optional
1   quart chicken stock (page 53) or canned low-sodium broth
1   cup half-and-half
4   green onions with some green tops, thinly sliced (½ cup)

1. In a 3½-quart or larger crockery slow-cooker set on HIGH, combine wild rice and oil. Stir to coat and cook, covered, for 15 minutes.

2. Change seeting to LOW if desired. Arrange leek, onion, and celery on top of rice. Add turkey pieces; season with herbs, pepper, and salt if desired. Pour in stock. Do not stir. Cover and cook for 7 to 8 hours on LOW or 3 to 3¾ hours on HIGH.

3. If cooking on LOW, return setting to HIGH. Stir in half-and-half. Cook, covered, for another 15 to 20 minutes, until heated through. Serve in individual soup bowls, sprinkled with thinly sliced green onions.

PREP TIME: 20 MIN

COOK TIME: 7–8 HR ON LOW + 30 MIN ON HIGH OR 3½–4¼ HR ON HIGH

Per serving: 362 calories, 37 g protein, 10 g total fat (3.7 g saturated), 32 g carbohydrates, 136 mg sodium, 92 mg cholesterol, 3 g dietary fiber

TURKEY CHOWDER

MAKES 4 SERVINGS

This is a delicious way to use the remains of the turkey from Thanksgiving when you have weekend guests and extra family to feed.

Serve the soup with crusty warm bread, green salad, and a cheese board. Make chocolate mousse for dessert, using your favorite recipe or a store-bought mix.

3   slices bacon, cut into ½-inch pieces
      and blanched in boiling water
2   medium red onions, chopped (2 cups)
2   large garlic cloves, minced
2   medium carrots, peeled
      and chopped (1½ cups)
2   medium celery ribs, thinly sliced (1 cup)
1   large red bell pepper, seeded
      and cut into ½-inch cubes (1½ cups)
1   pound butternut squash, peeled
      and cut into 1-inch cubes (4 cups)

½   tablespoon chopped fresh marjoram
      or ½ teaspoon dried, crumbled
½   tablespoon fresh thyme leaves
      or ½ teaspoon dried, crumbled
      Salt, optional, and freshly ground black
      pepper to taste
1   quart chicken stock (page 53) or canned
      low-sodium broth
1   10-ounce package frozen green peas
2   cups chopped skinless cooked turkey

**PREP TIME:
20 MIN**

**COOK TIME:
7–9 HR ON LOW +
15 MIN ON HIGH
OR 3³/₄–4³/₄ HR
ON HIGH**

1. Put all ingredients except stock, peas, and turkey in a 3½-quart or larger crockery slow-cooker, making layers in the order given. Pour in stock. Do not stir. Cover and cook on LOW for 7 to 9 hours or on HIGH for 3½ to 4½ hours.

2. Fifteen minutes before serving, add peas and turkey. If cooking on LOW, change setting to HIGH. Cover and cook until peas and turkey are heated through, about 15 minutes. Ladle into wide, shallow soup bowls.

Per serving: 353 calories, 33 g protein, 12 g total fat (3.9 g saturated), 30 g carbohydrates, 332 mg sodium, 61 mg cholesterol, 8 g dietary fiber

CHOLENT

MAKES 6 SERVINGS

In the Old Country, cholent was traditionally cooked overnight in communal ovens to be eaten at noon on the Jewish Sabbath, leading some scholars to believe that its name is derived from the French chaud, *meaning warm. Others claim the name comes from the Yiddish* shul ende, *the end of synagogue, since that is when the meat and vegetable stew was eaten. There are many Heartland recipes for this savory dish—this version is particularly easy to make in a crockery slow-cooker.*

If using a 3½- or 4-quart slow-cooker, prepare half of the recipe.

1½ cups dried lima beans, rinsed and picked over
6 cups water
2 large yellow onions, sliced (4 cups)
¼ cup barley
2 large garlic cloves, sliced
1 2½- to 3-pound beef brisket

1 large tomato, quartered
2 large celery ribs, quartered
1½ cups tomato juice
2 teaspoons hot paprika
½ teaspoon freshly ground black pepper
Salt, optional

**PREP TIME:
15 MIN + AT
LEAST 1¼ HR FOR
SOAKING BEANS**

**COOK TIME:
10–12 HR ON LOW
OR 6–7 HR
ON HIGH**

1. In a 5-quart or larger crockery slow-cooker, soak beans in water overnight or for at least 6 hours. Or put beans and water in a large pot and bring to a boil on top of the stove. Boil for 2 minutes, turn off heat, and let stand 1 hour. Drain beans and place in the slow-cooker. Stir in onions, barley, and garlic.

2. Trim excess fat from brisket. If necessary, cut brisket to fit into slow-cooker. Lay brisket on top of beans. Top with tomato and celery. Combine tomato juice, paprika, and pepper. Pour over brisket. Do not stir. Cover and cook on LOW for 10 to 12 hours or on HIGH for 6 to 7 hours. Season with salt to taste.

3. Transfer brisket to a carving board and thinly slice. Serve with the vegetables and natural pan juices.

Per serving: 544 calories, 55 g protein, 16 g total fat (5.6 g saturated), 44 g carbohydrates, 410 mg sodium, 129 mg cholesterol, 11 g dietary fiber

COUNTRY CHICKEN STEW
WITH BASIL DUMPLINGS

MAKES 6 SERVINGS

When I was growing up, my mother kept a large flock of chickens, laying hens for fresh eggs and a steady supply of broiler-fryers for great chicken dishes like this homey stew.

12 small white onions	⅓ cup dry white wine
Water	2 tablespoons unbleached all-purpose flour
1 pound boneless, skinless chicken thighs	2 tablespoons butter, at room temperature
1 pound boneless, skinless chicken breast halves	1 pound fresh asparagus, trimmed and cut
½ tablespoon chopped fresh basil leaves	into 1½-inch lengths
or ½ teaspoon dried, crumbled	DUMPLINGS
Salt, optional, and freshly ground	1 cup buttermilk biscuit and baking mix
black pepper to taste	⅓ cup whole milk
1 large red bell pepper, seeded and cut into	¼ cup chopped fresh basil leaves
1-inch squares (1½ cups)	or 1 tablespoon dried, crumbled
4 large garlic cloves, thinly sliced	
2 cups chicken stock (page 53) or canned	
low-sodium broth	

PREP TIME: 25 MIN

COOK TIME: 6–8 HR ON LOW + 30 MIN ON HIGH OR 2½–3 HR ON HIGH

1. Using a sharp knife, make a small X in the root end of each onion. Bring a saucepan of water to a boil. Add the onions, lower the heat, and simmer for 5 minutes. Drain and rinse under running cold water. Slip skins off onions.

2. Rinse chicken and pat dry. Quarter the thighs and chicken breast halves. Stir in basil and season with salt and pepper.

3. Put chicken pieces in a 3½-quart or larger crockery slow-cooker. Top with onions, bell pepper, and garlic. Pour in stock and wine. Do not stir. Cover and cook on LOW for 6 to 8 hours or on HIGH for 2 to 2½ hours.

4. Stir the stew. If cooking on LOW, change setting to HIGH. In a small bowl, blend together the flour and butter. Stir into slow-cooker. Cook, stirring, until sauce begins to thicken, about 5 minutes. Stir in asparagus.

5. In a medium bowl, combine dumpling ingredients until evenly moistened. Drop by tablespoons onto hot stew in 6 small mounds. Cover and cook for another 25 to 30 minutes, until dumplings are cooked through. Serve immediately.

Per serving: 373 calories, 39 g protein, 12 g total fat (4.5 g saturated), 25 g carbohydrates, 512 mg sodium, 119 mg cholesterol, 3 g dietary fiber

COWBOY STEW OVER CREAMY POLENTA

MAKES 4 SERVINGS

A hearty beef stew filled with simple, homey goodness. It's doubtful that "trail grub" was ever this delicious! The stew is also excellent served with mashed yellow turnips. If you're not familiar with fresh chile peppers, see page 19.

Polenta is better known in the Heartland as cornmeal mush. We ate a lot of it when I was growing up, cooked until firm, cut into squares, and fried. I like to serve this stew over the polenta when it has the consistency of grits.

1 large yellow onion, chopped (1½ cups)
1 large garlic clove, minced
1 jalapeño chile pepper, seeded and minced (1 tablespoon)
1 Anaheim chile pepper, seeded and minced (¼ cup)
1 large red bell pepper, seeded and cut into 1-inch squares (1½ cups)
2 tablespoons unbleached all-purpose flour
½ teaspoon ground cumin
¼ teaspoon lemon pepper seasoning
1 teaspoon chili powder
1 teaspoon chopped fresh oregano leaves or ¼ teaspoon dried, crumbled
1 teaspoon chopped fresh thyme leaves or ¼ teaspoon dried, crumbled
1 pound lean beef stew meat, cut into 1-inch cubes

4 tomatillos, husked, rinsed, and coarsely chopped (1 cup)
1 14½-ounce can Italian plum tomatoes, undrained
1 cup beef stock (page 82) or canned low-sodium broth
½ cup dry red wine
2 tablespoons tomato paste
2 medium zucchini, halved lengthwise and cut into 1-inch slices (2 cups)

CREAMY POLENTA

1 quart water
Dash salt
1 cup instant polenta or stone-ground yellow cornmeal
2 tablespoons freshly grated Parmesan cheese
1 tablespoon butter

PREP TIME: 30 MIN

COOK TIME: 9–10 HR ON LOW OR 4½–5 HR ON HIGH

1. Place onion and garlic in a 3½-quart or larger crockery slow-cooker. Top with peppers.

2. In a self-sealing plastic bag, shake flour, spices, and herbs to combine. Add beef cubes and shake to coat evenly. Place meat on top of vegetables in slow-cooker.

3. Cover meat with tomatillos and tomatoes with their juice. Combine stock, wine, and tomato paste. Pour over all. Do not stir. Cook on LOW for 8½ to 9½ hours or on HIGH for 4¼ to 4¾ hours.

4. Add zucchini and stir the stew. Cover and cook on LOW for 30 minutes or on HIGH for 15 minutes.

5. Just before serving, bring water and salt for polenta to a rapid boil in a 2-quart nonstick saucepan. Sprinkle instant polenta over boiling water. Reduce heat to medium and cook, stirring constantly, until polenta is thick and creamy, about 5 minutes. Stir Parmesan cheese and butter into polenta.

6. Spoon polenta into one side of each of 4 wide, shallow soup bowls. Stir stew and ladle alongside polenta. Serve at once.

Per serving: 455 calories, 31 g protein, 14 g total fat (5.6 g saturated), 48 g carbohydrates, 558 mg sodium, 80 mg cholesterol, 7 g dietary fiber

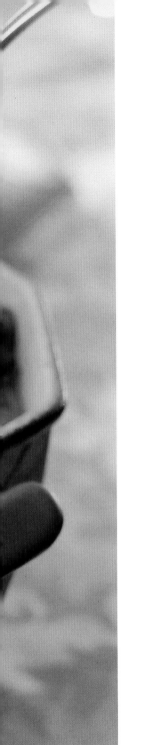

LAMB AND BUTTERNUT SQUASH STEW

MAKES 6 SERVINGS

Lamb was not popular when I was growing up in the Midwest. Today lamb farms abound in several states in the Heartland, making this delicious red meat more readily available. This is a particularly delectable way to prepare it.

If using a 3½- or 4-quart slow-cooker, prepare half of the recipe.

¼ cup unbleached all-purpose flour Salt, optional	2 medium celery ribs, chopped (1 cup)
½ teaspoon freshly ground black pepper	4 large garlic cloves, thinly sliced
¼ teaspoon ground cloves	1 large white potato, scrubbed and cubed (1½ cups)
¼ teaspoon ground nutmeg	1 14½-ounce can whole peeled tomatoes, juices drained and reserved
2 pounds boneless leg of lamb, cut into 2-inch cubes	1 butternut squash (about 1½ pounds)
1 tablespoon olive oil	1 cup beef stock (page 82) or canned low-sodium broth
2 medium yellow onions, chopped (2 cups)	2 large bay leaves
2 medium carrots, peeled and chopped (1½ cups)	¾ cup raisins

PREP TIME: 30 MIN

COOK TIME: 8–10 HR ON LOW OR 4–5 HR ON HIGH

1. In a self-sealing plastic bag, shake flour, salt, pepper, cloves, and nutmeg to combine. Add lamb and shake to coat evenly. In a large skillet, heat oil over medium-high heat. Add lamb and cook for 5 minutes, turning lamb pieces frequently to brown on all sides.

2. Transfer lamb to a 5-quart or larger crockery slow-cooker. Top with onions, carrots, celery, and garlic. Place potato and tomatoes around sides.

3. Cut squash in half lengthwise and remove seeds. Peel squash and cut each half into 4 pieces. Place squash, cut side down, on top of lamb. Pour stock and reserved tomato juices over squash. Add bay leaves and raisins. Do not stir. Cover and cook on LOW for 8 to 10 hours or on HIGH for 4 to 5 hours. Discard bay leaves. If cooking on HIGH, stir stew once during last hour of cooking.

4. To serve, spoon stew into wide, shallow soup bowls.

Per serving: 427 calories, 36 g protein, 12 g total fat (3.5 g saturated), 47 g carbohydrates, 228 mg sodium, 97 mg cholesterol, 6 g dietary fiber

MEATBALL STEW

MAKES 4 SERVINGS

I especially like this recipe because it can easily be adjusted to fit your family's tastes or what you have on hand. When my sons were very young, I used Italian seasoning in the meatballs and fresh carrots and frozen peas as the vegetables, adding the peas during the last 30 minutes of cooking time.

Once they developed a taste for spicier foods, the following version was a guaranteed hit. Round out the meal with a tossed salad, a loaf of crusty bread, and a fruit dessert.

1 cup long-grain white rice
8 small white onions, about ½ pound
  Water
1 pound lean ground beef round
1 small russet potato, peeled and shredded (½ cup)
1 small yellow onion, chopped (½ cup)
2 large garlic cloves, minced
1 teaspoon chili powder
½ teaspoon ground cumin
½ tablespoon chopped fresh oregano leaves or ½ teaspoon dried, crumbled

Salt, optional
½ teaspoon freshly ground black pepper
1 Anaheim chile pepper, seeded and minced (¼ cup)
1 large green bell pepper, seeded and cut into 1-inch squares (1½ cups)
1 large red bell pepper, seeded and cut into 1-inch pieces (1½ cups)
1 32-ounce can vegetable juice

PREP TIME: 30 MIN

COOK TIME: 6–8 HR ON LOW OR 3–4 HR ON HIGH

1. Put rice in a 3½-quart or larger crockery slow-cooker. Cut an X in the root end of each white onion. Put onions in a medium saucepan with water to cover. Bring to a quick boil. Reduce heat to medium-high and cook for 2 minutes. Drain and rinse with cold running water. Slip off onion skins. (If cooking on HIGH, cut each onion in half.) Add onions to slow-cooker.

2. In a large bowl, combine remaining ingredients except peppers and juice. Mix well. Form into 1½-inch meatballs (you should get about 16). Place meatballs on top of rice. Arrange peppers on top. Pour vegetable juice over all. Do not stir. Cover and cook on LOW for 6 to 8 hours or on HIGH for 3 to 4 hours. If cooking on HIGH, stir stew once during last hour of cooking.

3. Stir before serving.

Per serving: 487 calories, 31 g protein, 11 g total fat (4.3 g saturated), 66 g carbohydrates, 981 mg sodium, 41 mg cholesterol, 6 g dietary fiber

PORK STEW

MAKES 4 SERVINGS

This is a fabulous pork dish, and the slow-cooking intensifies the flavors. Serve it with mashed potatoes and shredded steamed green cabbage dressed with butter and lemon juice.

1½ pounds boneless pork loin, cut into ½-inch cubes

1 tablespoon mild vegetable oil, such as canola

1 medium yellow onion, quartered and thinly sliced (1½ cups)

4 green onions, including some green tops, thinly sliced (½ cup)

1 medium green bell pepper, seeded and chopped (1 cup)

2 medium carrots, peeled and chopped (1½ cups)

2 medium celery ribs, chopped (1 cup)

1 14½-ounce can whole tomatoes, juices drained and reserved

3 large garlic cloves, minced

¾ cup dry white wine

½ cup water

1 tablespoon Worcestershire sauce

½ tablespoon chopped fresh marjoram leaves or ½ teaspoon dried, crumbled
Salt, optional, and freshly ground black pepper to taste

PREP TIME: 20 MIN

COOK TIME: 7-9 HR ON LOW OR 3½-4½ HR ON HIGH

1. In a large skillet, brown pork in oil over medium-high heat for 5 minutes, turning pieces to brown all sides.

2. Transfer pork to a 3½-quart or larger crockery slow-cooker and top with yellow onion, green onions, bell pepper, carrots, and celery. Layer tomatoes and garlic on top.

3. In a medium bowl, whisk together reserved tomato juice, wine, water, Worcestershire sauce, marjoram, salt, and pepper. Pour over pork and vegetables. Do not stir. Cover and cook on LOW for 7 to 9 hours or on HIGH for 3½ to 4½ hours. If cooking on HIGH, stir stew once during last hour of cooking.

4. To serve, stir the stew and ladle into wide, shallow soup bowls.

Per serving: 441 calories, 37 g protein, 22 g total fat (6.7 g saturated), 16 g carbohydrates, 318 mg sodium, 99 mg cholesterol, 3 g dietary fiber

PRAIRIE RABBIT STEW WITH WILD MUSHROOMS

MAKES 6 SERVINGS

Rabbit has a flavor similar to chicken and is very low in cholesterol. Frozen rabbit is available year-round in larger supermarkets through much of the Heartland. Thaw it overnight in the refrigerator. This is also excellent made with chicken.

Serve over wide egg noodles and garnish with fresh rosemary if desired.

1 3-pound rabbit, thawed if frozen, quartered
  Salt, optional, and freshly ground
  black pepper to taste
1 tablespoon olive oil
  Strips of rind from ½ orange, removed with a
  vegetable peeler
1 tablespoon chopped fresh rosemary leaves
  or 1 teaspoon dried, crumbled
1 large garlic clove, minced

½ teaspoon crushed red pepper
1 10-ounce package frozen white pearl onions
1 large tomato, peeled, seeded, and chopped
  (1½ cups)
½ pound wild mushrooms (morels, shiitake,
  or porcini), cleaned and sliced (6 cups)
1 cup dry white wine
2 tablespoons unbleached all-purpose flour,
  optional

**PREP TIME:
20 MIN**

**COOK TIME:
7–9 HR ON LOW +
OPTIONAL 15 MIN ON
HIGH OR 2¼–3 HR
+ OPTIONAL 15 MIN
ON HIGH**

1. Rinse rabbit pieces and pat dry. Season with salt and pepper. In a large heavy skillet, brown rabbit pieces in oil over medium-high heat for 5 minutes, turning to brown both sides.

2. Transfer rabbit to a 3½-quart or larger crockery slow-cooker. Sprinkle with orange rind, rosemary, garlic, and crushed red pepper. Scatter onions and tomato around the rabbit. Top with mushrooms. Pour in wine. Do not stir. Cover and cook on LOW for 7 to 9 hours or on HIGH for 2¼ to 3 hours.

3. Remove rabbit from slow-cooker. Cut the rabbit meat off the bones, coarsely chop, and return meat to stew. If desired, thicken the stew by making a smooth paste of the flour and ¼ cup juices from the stew. Stir into slow-cooker. Cover and cook until thickened, about 15 minutes, changing setting to HIGH if cooking on LOW.

4. To serve, ladle into wide, shallow soup bowls.

Per serving: 351 calories, 40 g protein, 13 g total fat (3.5 g saturated), 10 g carbohydrates, 70 mg sodium, 107 mg cholesterol, 2 g dietary fiber

SPICY PORK RAGOUT

MAKES 4 SERVINGS

Since pork is a very lean meat, I serve it at least once a week. This ragout is served with steamed rice and heated canned black beans. Offer a salad of crisp romaine lettuce leaves, sliced oranges, and sliced black olives drizzled with a little vinaigrette.

2 pounds boneless pork loin, cut into
    1½-inch pieces
¾ cup fresh orange juice
¼ cup fresh lime juice
1 large yellow onion, chopped (1½ cups)
2 large garlic cloves, minced
1 4-ounce can diced green chiles, drained
1 tablespoon chopped fresh oregano leaves
    or 1 teaspoon dried, crumbled

1 teaspoon ground cumin
1 teaspoon paprika
¼ teaspoon cayenne pepper
¼ teaspoon freshly ground black pepper
2 cups hot cooked rice
1 15½-ounce can black beans, heated
    and drained
    Sliced green onions for garnish

PREP TIME:
20 MIN

COOK TIME:
7–9 HR ON LOW
OR 3½–4½ HR
ON HIGH

1. Put pork in a 3½-quart or larger crockery slow-cooker. In a large bowl, combine remaining ingredients except rice, beans, and green onions and pour over pork. Do not stir. Cover and cook on LOW for 7 to 9 hours or on HIGH for 3½ to 4½ hours. If cooking on HIGH, stir ragout once during last hour of cooking.

2. To serve, ladle the stew into one side of individual wide, shallow soup bowls. Spoon rice and black beans into the bowls. Do not mix. Garnish with sliced green onions.

Per serving: 567 calories, 57 g protein, 14 g total fat (4.5 g saturated), 51 g carbohydrates, 440 mg sodium, 134 mg cholesterol, 7 g dietary fiber

VENISON STEW WITH DRIED CHERRIES

MAKES 6 SERVINGS

If you don't have access to fresh venison, you can order it by mail (see Sources, page 142). This stew calls for dried cherries, which are also available by mail order, at larger supermarkets, and at natural foods stores. Most dried cherries come from Michigan, where more than 85 million pounds of tart cherries are grown annually— an industry that started from a one-acre cherry orchard planted in the 1880s.

Serve the stew with steamed new potatoes sprinkled with parsley and a green salad or a green vegetable in a vinaigrette.

¼ cup unbleached all-purpose flour

1 tablespoon chopped fresh thyme leaves or 1 teaspoon dried, crumbled
Salt, optional, and freshly ground black pepper to taste

3 pounds boneless venison stew meat from the leg, cut into 1-inch pieces

2 tablespoons olive oil

2 medium carrots, peeled and chopped (1½ cups)

3 medium celery ribs, chopped (1½ cups)

1 large yellow onion, chopped (1½ cups)

3 large garlic cloves, chopped

1 cup beef stock (page 82) or canned low-sodium broth

1 cup dry red wine

¼ cup tomato paste

3 tablespoons fresh orange juice

½ cup dried cherries

¼ cup brandy

1. In a self-sealing plastic bag, shake flour, thyme, salt, and pepper to combine. Add venison and shake to coat evenly. In a large skillet, brown venison in oil over medium-high heat on all sides, about 5 minutes.

2. In a 3½-quart or larger crockery slow-cooker, combine venison, carrots, celery, onion, and garlic. In a medium bowl, whisk together stock, wine, tomato paste, and orange juice. Pour over venison. Do not stir. Cover and cook on LOW for 7 to 9 hours or on HIGH for 3½ to 4½ hours.

3. Add cherries and brandy; stir to combine. Cover and cook for another hour if cooking on LOW or another 30 minutes if cooking on HIGH.

4. To serve, ladle into wide, shallow soup plates.

PREP TIME: 25 MIN

COOK TIME: 8-10 HR ON LOW OR 4-5 HR ON HIGH

Per serving: 466 calories, 58 g protein, 11 g total fat (3.2 g saturated), 21 g carbohydrates, 753 mg sodium, 205 mg cholesterol, 2 g dietary fiber

WISCONSIN DUCK STEW

MAKES 6 SERVINGS

Wild ducks are the prize of the hunter in most every Heartland state, but in Wisconsin ducks are a profitable industry. You can order duck breast by mail (see Sources, page 142) or you can substitute chicken or turkey breast in this extraordinary stew. The duck breasts need to marinate in an herb paste for several hours (or overnight), so plan accordingly.

3   8-ounce boneless duck breasts

HERB MARINADE

2   tablespoons balsamic vinegar

2   large garlic cloves, peeled

½   tablespoon fresh thyme leaves
    or ½ teaspoon dried, crumbled

1   teaspoon chopped fresh rosemary
    leaves or ¼ teaspoon dried, crumbled
    Salt, optional, and freshly ground
    black pepper

STEW

3   large celery ribs with leaves, chopped
    (4 cups)

2   medium leeks with 1 inch pale green
    top, well rinsed and chopped (1½ cups)

4   small red-skinned potatoes, scrubbed
    and cut into ½-inch cubes (1½ cups)

1   medium yellow onion, chopped
    (1 cup)

1   medium carrot, peeled and chopped
    (¾ cup)

2   tablespoons butter

2   tablespoons unbleached all-purpose flour

1½ cups chicken stock (page 53)
    or canned low-sodium broth

1   teaspoon fresh thyme leaves
    or ¼ teaspoon dried, crumbled

1   tablespoon tomato paste

½   pound fresh morels (6 cups) or button
    mushrooms, thinly sliced (2½ cups)

1. Remove skin and excess fat from duck breasts. In a food processor or blender, puree marinade ingredients to form a paste. Rub into duck breasts and wrap securely in plastic wrap. Chill for at least 6 hours or overnight.

PREP TIME: 25 MIN +6 HR FOR MARINATING

COOK TIME: 6–8 HR ON LOW OR 2½–3¼ HR ON HIGH

2. When ready to cook, cut duck breasts into 1½-inch cubes. In a 3½-quart or larger crockery slow-cooker, combine duck pieces with celery, leeks, potatoes, onion, and carrot.

3. In a medium saucepan, melt butter over medium heat. Stir in flour and cook, stirring constantly, until mixture begins to brown. Whisk in stock; add thyme and tomato paste. Stir mixture into the slow-cooker. Cover and cook on LOW for 5½ to 7½ hours or on HIGH for 2¼ to 3 hours.

4. Stir in mushrooms. Cook, covered, for 30 minutes if cooking on LOW, 15 minutes if cooking on HIGH.

5. To serve, ladle into wide, shallow soup bowls.

Per serving: 253 calories, 23 g protein, 9 g total fat (3.8 g saturated), 21 g carbohydrates, 167 mg sodium, 83 mg cholesterol, 3 g dietary fiber

POULTRY
AND GAME

AS NEW FLAVORS AND FOODS HAVE BECOME more readily available through the supermarkets of the Heartland, the way we cook chicken and other forms of poultry and game has changed significantly. When I was growing up in Kansas, the chicken was either baked, fried, or stewed, and the seasonings rarely changed its mild flavor.

Today boneless breasts (chicken and turkey) are available in the smallest of grocery stores, and the Cornish game hen, once a restaurant item only, is readily available in most areas. Most of my recipes are for chicken, but you'll also find new and exciting ways to prepare game hens, turkey breast, duck, pheasant, and rabbit. The recipes are inspired by a variety of eras and reflect the growing influence of the world on Heartland cooking.

Start your recipes off right by using the best poultry and game that you can buy. I purchase free-range poultry from a nearby farmer's market—the flavor is far superior to mass-produced birds.

Another secret that makes the difference between a good dish and a great one, is the use of fresh herbs in these recipes. You don't need a garden to grow herbs; even a sunny apartment windowsill can produce plenty of basil, rosemary, sage, savory, and thyme.

CHICKEN
IN THE POT

MAKES 4 SERVINGS

In earlier days when the Heartland was being settled, most homes had a vegetable patch. Nowadays, if there's a kitchen garden, there is also very likely an herb garden.

This savory chicken dish has lots of fresh herbs tucked under the chicken skin for added flavor. Serve it with mashed sweet potatoes seasoned with butter, thyme, and a little freshly grated nutmeg.

If using a 3½- or 4-quart slow-cooker, cut chicken into serving pieces.

1 3- to 3½-pound chicken
3 sprigs fresh basil leaves
   or ½ teaspoon dried, crumbled
2 sprigs fresh flat-leaf parsley
1 large lemon, cut in half
3 medium leeks, white part only, well
   rinsed and cut in half lengthwise

12 large garlic cloves, peeled
12 shallots, peeled
1 cup chicken stock (page 53) or
   canned low-sodium broth
½ cup dry white wine

**PREP TIME:
25 MIN

COOK TIME:
6–8 HR ON LOW OR
2¼–2¾ ON HIGH

STANDING TIME:
10 MIN**

1. Rinse chicken and pat dry. Discard neck and giblets or reserve for another use. Using your fingers and working from the neck cavity, separate skin from breast meat without tearing skin. Tuck basil and parsley under skin over the breast meat. Place lemon halves in body cavity and tie drumsticks together with kitchen string.

2. Place a metal rack or trivet in a 5-quart or larger crockery slow-cooker. Arrange leeks on top of rack and place chicken, breast side up, on top of leeks. Surround chicken with garlic and shallots. Pour in stock and wine. Cover and cook on LOW for 6 to 8 hours or on HIGH for 2¼ to 2¾ hours.

3. To serve, transfer chicken and vegetables to a heated serving platter. Discard lemon and string. Let rest for 10 minutes before carving. Pass pan juices in a gravy boat to spoon on each serving.

Per serving: 461 calories, 45 g protein, 22 g total fat (6.0 g saturated), 15 g carbohydrates, 145 mg sodium, 131 mg cholesterol, 3 g dietary fiber

CHICKEN STOCK

MAKES 2 QUARTS NON-REDUCED STOCK

PREP TIME: 20 MIN • COOK TIME: 7–10 HR ON LOW • OR 3½–5 HR ON HIGH

I depend on this richly flavored stock for sauces and soups. Since I frequently buy whole chickens on sale to cut up for breasts and thighs, I freeze the rest. It doesn't take long to accumulate the necessary chicken parts. For an even richer flavor, boil the strained stock, uncovered, on top of the stove over high heat until it reduces by half.

1½	pounds chicken parts with bones, such as wings, legs, necks, and backs	2	quarts water
1	medium onion, peeled and stuck with 1 clove	3	peppercorns
1	large garlic clove, peeled	2	sprigs fresh flat-leaf parsley
1	large carrot, peeled and quartered	1	large bay leaf
1	large celery rib with leaves, quartered	1	sprig fresh thyme
		¼	teaspoon salt, optional

1. Put all ingredients in a 3½-quart or larger crockery slow-cooker. Cover and cook on LOW for 7 to 10 hours or on HIGH for 3½ to 5 hours, skimming off and discarding any foam that forms after the first 30 minutes of cooking time.

2. Strain stock through a fine sieve or a colander lined with cheesecloth; discard solids. If desired, cook stock in an uncovered saucepan on top of the stove over high heat until reduced by half. Store in a sealed container in refrigerator for as long as 3 days or freeze for up to 3 months, again skimming and discarding all fat that rises to the surface once the stock is chilled thoroughly.

Per 1-cup serving: 13 calories, trace protein, trace total fat (trace saturated), 39g carbohydrates, 46 mg sodium, 0 cholesterol, trace dietary fiber

CHICKEN WITH ORANGES AND WALNUTS

MAKES 4 SERVINGS

A chicken dish that combines three of my favorite flavors: orange, mint, and garlic. If you don't grow mint, you'll need to buy it at your supermarket. Or substitute another fresh herb such as cilantro or basil since dried mint simply won't impart the same flavor. Prepare this for a special dinner, mounded on a bed of fluffy rice.

1   3- to 3½-pound chicken, cut into serving pieces
1   tablespoon olive oil
2   thin-skinned oranges, such as Valencia, unpeeled, thinly sliced, seeds removed
3   large garlic cloves, thinly sliced
1   6-ounce can frozen orange juice concentrate, thawed
¼   cup dry sherry
¼   cup water
1   teaspoon chopped fresh thyme leaves or ¼ teaspoon dried, crumbled
2   tablespoons butter, at room temperature
2   tablespoons unbleached all-purpose flour
¼   cup chopped fresh mint
¼   cup finely chopped walnuts

PREP TIME: 25 MIN

COOK TIME: 6–8 HR ON LOW + 15 MIN ON HIGH OR 2¼–3 HR ON HIGH

1. Rinse chicken and pat dry. Discard giblets and neck or reserve for another use. In a large skillet, brown chicken pieces in oil over medium-high heat until golden, about 5 minutes per side.

2. Arrange chicken in a 3½-quart or larger crockery slow-cooker. Top with orange slices and garlic. In a medium bowl, combine orange juice concentrate, sherry, water, and thyme. Pour over chicken. Do not stir. Cover and cook on LOW for 6 to 8 hours or on HIGH for 2 to 2¾ hours. If cooking on HIGH, stir once during last half hour of cooking.

3. Transfer chicken and orange slices to a heated serving platter. Keep warm. In a small bowl, combine butter and flour. Whisk into pan juices in slow-cooker. If cooking on LOW, change setting to HIGH and cook, stirring, until thickened, about 10 minutes. Add mint and walnuts; cook for another 5 minutes. Spoon sauce over chicken and serve.

Per serving: 468 calories, 39 g protein, 19 g total fat (5.8 g saturated), 33 g carbohydrates, 190 mg sodium, 131 mg cholesterol, 2 g dietary fiber

CHICKEN WITH SUN-DRIED TOMATOES AND CILANTRO

MAKES 4 SERVINGS

This recipe calls for sun-dried tomatoes, but if your market doesn't carry them, use three sliced fresh plum tomatoes. Cilantro is a pungent herb. Most people love it with a passion, but there are a few who hate it. If you are one, substitute flat-leaf parsley or mint.

Serve this with sweet potatoes baked in their jackets and a fresh spinach and grapefruit salad.

2 pounds skinless, boneless chicken thighs	1 cup loosely packed fresh cilantro leaves
¼ pound oil-packed sun-dried tomatoes, drained of the oil and slivered lengthwise	¼ cup fresh lemon juice
	¼ cup dry white wine or water
4 large garlic cloves, thinly sliced	1 cup grated Monterey Jack cheese (¼ pound)

1. Rinse chicken and pat dry. Place half of the chicken pieces in a single layer in a 3½-quart or larger crockery slow-cooker. Top with half of the sun-dried tomatoes, half of the garlic, and half of the cilantro. Top with remaining chicken pieces, sun-dried tomatoes, garlic, and cilantro.

PREP TIME: 10 MIN

COOK TIME: 6–8 HR ON LOW + 15 MIN ON HIGH OR 2¼–3 HR ON HIGH

2. Sprinkle lemon juice over all; pour in wine. Do not stir. Cover and cook on LOW for 6 to 8 hours or on HIGH for 2 to 2¾ hours.

3. If cooking on LOW, change setting to HIGH. Sprinkle cheese over chicken, cover, and cook until cheese melts, about 15 minutes.

4. Transfer chicken and any pan juices to a heated serving platter.

Per serving: 440 calories, 53 g protein, 21 g total fat (8.1 g saturated), 8 g carbohydrates, 405 mg sodium, 213 mg cholesterol, 2 g dietary fiber

FRICASSEE OF CHICKEN AND VEGETABLES

MAKES 4 SERVINGS

An extravagantly delicious combination of flavors. Serve this in a ring mold of wild rice studded with golden raisins, toasted pecans, and a splash of dry sherry.

If using a 3½- or 4-quart slow-cooker, use 1½ to 2 pounds boneless chicken pieces instead of bone-in chicken pieces.

1	3- to 3½-pound chicken, cut into serving pieces	½	tablespoon chopped fresh tarragon leaves or ½ teaspoon dried, crumbled
	Salt, optional, and freshly ground black pepper to taste	4	medium carrots, peeled and cut into 2-inch pieces
1	tablespoon mild vegetable oil, such as canola	2	medium yellow onions, peeled and quartered
2	tablespoons butter	3	medium leeks, white part only, well rinsed and chopped (1½ cups)
2	large garlic cloves, minced	1	large bay leaf
2½	tablespoons unbleached all-purpose flour	½	cup half-and-half
2	cups chicken stock (page 53) or canned low-sodium broth	1	10-ounce package frozen peas, thawed and drained
1	tablespoon fresh thyme leaves or 1 teaspoon dried, crumbled		

PREP TIME:
25 MIN

COOK TIME:
6–8 HR ON LOW +
15 MIN ON HIGH
OR 2½–3 HR
ON HIGH

1. Rinse chicken and pat dry. Discard giblets and neck or reserve for another use. Season chicken with salt and pepper. In a large skillet, brown chicken in oil over medium-high heat until golden, about 5 minutes per side. Transfer chicken to a 5-quart or larger crockery slow-cooker.

2. Add butter to same skillet and reduce heat to low. Add garlic and sauté for 2 minutes. Stir in flour and cook for 1 minute. Whisk in stock. Stir in thyme and tarragon.

3. Add carrots, onions, and leeks to the slow-cooker. Pour stock mixture over all. Add bay leaf. Do not stir. Cover and cook on LOW for 6 to 8 hours or on HIGH for 2¼ to 2¾ hours. If cooking on HIGH, stir once during last half hour of cooking.

4. If cooking on LOW, change setting to HIGH. Stir in half-and-half and peas. Cover and cook for another 15 minutes, until peas are heated through.

5. To serve, discard bay leaf. Arrange chicken pieces and vegetables on a serving platter and spoon sauce over top.

Per serving: 495 calories, 45 g protein, 19 g total fat (7.6 g saturated), 35 g carbohydrates, 351 mg sodium, 142 mg cholesterol, 8 g dietary fiber

HERBED LEMON CHICKEN AND RICE

MAKES 4 SERVINGS

Ideal for Sunday dinner, this herbed chicken is easy to assemble. The chicken marinates in fresh lemon juice for several hours (or overnight) before cooking so the fresh lemon flavor nicely infuses the chicken.

Another time, try a different combination of fresh herbs, such as thyme, savory, and rosemary.

If using a 3½- or 4-quart slow-cooker, use 1½ to 2 pounds boneless chicken pieces instead of bone-in chicken pieces.

1 3- to 3½-pound chicken, quartered	Salt, optional, and freshly ground black pepper to taste
3 large garlic cloves, sliced	
1½ cups fresh lemon juice, about 8 large lemons	1 cup mixed chopped fresh herbs such as dill, mint, and flat-leaf parsley
¼ cup unbleached all-purpose flour	1¾ cups chicken stock (page 53) or canned low-sodium broth
½ tablespoon hot paprika	
1 tablespoon olive oil	
1 cup long-grain white rice	
1 medium yellow onion, thinly sliced (1½ cups)	

PREP TIME: 15 MIN + AT LEAST 6 HR FOR MARINATING

COOK TIME: 6–8 HR ON LOW OR 2¼–3 HR ON HIGH

1. Rinse chicken and pat dry. Discard giblets and neck or reserve for another use. Put chicken pieces and garlic in a shallow glass dish and pour lemon juice over all. Cover with plastic wrap and refrigerate for at least 6 hours or overnight, turning chicken pieces occasionally.

2. When ready to cook, drain chicken, reserving lemon juice and garlic. In a large self-sealing plastic bag, shake flour and paprika to combine. Add a chicken quarter and shake to coat evenly. Repeat until all chicken pieces are dredged in flour mixture.

3. In a large nonstick skillet, brown chicken pieces in oil over medium-high heat until golden, about 5 minutes per side. Remove chicken and keep warm.

4. Put rice in a 5-quart or larger crockery slow-cooker and top with onion and chicken.

5. In a small saucepan, whisk together reserved lemon juice and garlic, salt, pepper, herbs, and stock. Bring to a full boil and boil for 1 minute. Pour over chicken. Do not stir. Cover and cook on LOW for 6 to 8 hours or on HIGH for 2¼ to 3 hours.

6. Transfer chicken and rice to a heated serving platter.

Per serving: 482 calories, 43 g protein, 10 g total fat (2.1 g saturated), 55 g carbohydrates, 168 mg sodium, 115 mg cholesterol, 2 g dietary fiber

PAPRIKA STUFFED CHICKEN BREASTS

MAKES 4 SERVINGS

This recipe is adapted from one given to me years ago by my sister-in-law, Gloria. Stuffed with mushrooms, shallots, and fresh dill, it's perfect for company.

Serve the chicken with roasted new potatoes and lightly steamed fiddleheads, topped with crumbled crisp-cooked bacon. The coiled tips of young fern fronds, fiddleheads have a flavor often described as a cross between asparagus and a woodsy mushroom. Each spring they are harvested in the forests of Michigan and Minnesota to be sold fresh in larger supermarkets or specialty produce stores throughout the Heartland. The rest of the year, look for them frozen. If you can't find them, substitute asparagus or another green vegetable.

4 tablespoons butter	Salt, optional, and freshly ground black pepper to taste
½ pound fresh morels or porcini mushrooms, finely chopped (4 cups)	½ cup dry white wine
2 shallots, chopped	1 tablespoon Worcestershire sauce
1 tablespoon dry sherry	1 large garlic clove, minced
3 tablespoons chopped fresh dill or 1 tablespoon dried dill weed	1½ tablespoons sweet paprika
	1 cup sour cream
2 large boneless, skinless whole chicken breasts, halved lengthwise (about 2 pounds total)	3 tablespoons unbleached all-purpose flour
	1 tablespoon tomato paste

PREP TIME:
25 MIN

COOK TIME:
6–8 HR ON LOW +
15 MIN ON HIGH
OR 2¼–3 HR
ON HIGH

1. In a small skillet, melt 2 tablespoons of the butter over medium-low heat. Add mushrooms, shallots, and sherry. Sauté, stirring occasionally, until mixture is almost dry, about 10 minutes. Remove from heat and stir in dill.

2. Meanwhile, pound each chicken breast half between 2 pieces of plastic wrap or waxed paper until thin. Place one-fourth of the mushroom mixture in the center of each chicken breast. Tuck in sides and roll up jelly-roll style, pressing to seal well.

3. In a large skillet, melt remaining 2 tablespoons butter over medium heat. Season chicken rolls with salt and pepper and sauté in butter until browned on all sides, about 5 minutes per side. Using a slotted spoon, transfer chicken rolls, seam side down, to a 3½-quart or larger crockery slow-cooker. Add wine, Worcestershire sauce, and garlic to skillet and stir, scraping to remove brown bits. Pour wine mixture over chicken rolls. Sprinkle with paprika. Cover and cook on LOW for 6 to 8 hours or on HIGH for 2 to 2¾ hours. If cooking on HIGH, stir once during last half hour of cooking.

4. Transfer chicken rolls to a heated platter; keep warm. If cooking on LOW, change setting to HIGH. In a small bowl, combine sour cream, flour, and tomato paste. Add to slow-cooker and stir well. Return chicken rolls to slow-cooker and spoon sauce over them to coat thoroughly. Cover and continue to cook for another 15 minutes.

5. To serve, transfer chicken and sauce to a heated serving platter.

Per serving: 554 calories, 57 g protein, 27 g total fat (15.5 g saturated), 15 g carbohydrates, 376 mg sodium, 188 mg cholesterol, 2 g dietary fiber

POACHED CHICKEN WITH VEGETABLES

MAKES 4 SERVINGS

With this recipe the humble chicken is elevated into something special. Serve this over cooked Homemade Noodles (page 31) or fresh fettuccine tossed with butter and a pinch of saffron.

1 large green bell pepper, seeded and cut into thin strips (1½ cups)

4 green onions, including some green tops, sliced (½ cup)

¼ pound fresh button mushrooms, sliced (1¼ cups)

1 3- to 3½-pound chicken, cut into serving pieces

Salt, optional, and freshly ground black pepper to taste

½ tablespoon chopped fresh oregano leaves or ½ teaspoon dried, crumbled

1 4-ounce jar whole pimientos, cut into thin strips (¼ cup)

½ cup chopped fresh flat-leaf parsley

1 cup dry white wine

PREP TIME: 20 MIN

COOK TIME: 6–8 HR ON LOW OR 2¼–2¾ HR ON HIGH

1. Put green pepper in a 3½-quart or larger crockery slow-cooker. Top with green onions and mushrooms.

2. Rinse chicken and pat dry. Discard giblets and neck or reserve for another use. Arrange chicken pieces on top of vegetables. Season with salt, pepper, and oregano. Top with pimientos. Sprinkle with parsley and pour in wine. Do not stir. Cover and cook on LOW for 6 to 8 hours or on HIGH for 2¼ to 2¾ hours.

3. To serve, arrange chicken and vegetables on a heated serving platter. Spoon any pan juices over top.

Per serving: 264 calories, 37 g protein, 5 g total fat (1.4 g saturated), 7 g carbohydrates, 140 mg sodium, 115 mg cholesterol, 2 g dietary fiber

SPICY GLAZED CHICKEN

MAKES 6 SERVINGS

This simple-to-prepare dish wraps up beautifully in warmed flour or corn tortillas along with avocado slices, sour cream, and sprigs of fresh cilantro. Be sure to buy a good-quality jalapeño jelly with plenty of heat. ▶

SPICY GLAZED CHICKEN *(see previous page for photo and notes)*

2 pounds boneless, skinless chicken breasts
¼ cup fresh orange juice (about 1 small orange)
1 cup drained canned water-packed pineapple bits
⅓ cup jalapeño chile pepper jelly
1 tablespoon freshly grated orange rind
1 tablespoon chopped fresh oregano leaves or 1 teaspoon dried, crumbled
1 large garlic clove, minced
½ teaspoon ground cumin
Salt, optional, and freshly ground black pepper to taste
12 7-inch flour or corn tortillas, fresh or frozen, thawed
1 large ripe avocado, peeled, pitted, and thinly sliced
½ cup sour cream
Sprigs fresh cilantro for garnish

PREP TIME: 15 MIN

COOK TIME: 6–7 HR ON LOW OR 2–2³/₄ HR ON HIGH

1. Rinse chicken and pat dry. Cut into thin lengthwise strips and put in a 3½-quart or larger crockery slow-cooker.

2. In a small saucepan, combine orange juice, pineapple, jalapeño jelly, orange rind, oregano, garlic, cumin, salt, and pepper. Cook over low heat, stirring, until jelly dissolves. Spoon over chicken. Stir to combine well. Cover and cook on LOW for 6 to 7 hours or on HIGH for 2 to 2¾ hours. If cooking on HIGH, stir once during last half hour of cooking.

3. To warm tortillas, preheat oven to 350°F. Wrap tortillas in foil and heat for 10 to 15 minutes or until hot and softened. Place avocado, sour cream, and cilantro sprigs in small serving bowls.

4. Spoon chicken and some of the pan juices onto tortillas, adding avocado, sour cream, and cilantro. Roll up tortillas.

Per serving (2 filled tortillas): 507 calories, 42 g protein, 15 g total fat (3.8 g saturated), 53 g carbohydrates, 429 mg sodium, 96 mg cholesterol, 2 g dietary fiber

SAVORY SUNDAY CHICKEN DINNER

MAKES 4 SERVINGS

In earlier times Sunday in the Heartland often meant fried chicken—delicious, but loaded with calories. This savory whole-meal chicken dish leaves out the fat but not the flavor!

Pass lemon wedges to squeeze over each serving. Add a fresh green salad and a simple fruit dessert, and your menu's complete.

If using a 3½- or 4-quart slow-cooker, use 1½ to 2 pounds boneless chicken pieces instead of bone-in chicken pieces.

1 3- to 3½-pound chicken, cut into serving pieces	½ pound fresh green beans, trimmed
1 tablespoon olive oil	¼ cup chicken stock (page 53) or canned low-sodium broth
2 medium yellow onions, chopped (2 cups)	½ tablespoon chopped fresh thyme leaves or ½ teaspoon dried, crumbled
1 large garlic clove, minced	1 teaspoon chopped fresh rosemary leaves or ¼ teaspoon dried, crumbled
1 tablespoon chopped fresh flat-leaf parsley	
1 pound small new potatoes, scrubbed and halved	2 medium leeks, white part only, well rinsed and cut into julienne strips (1 cup)
1 large yellow turnip, peeled and cut into 8 pieces	2 tablespoons balsamic vinegar
4 large plum tomatoes (about 1 pound total)	1 fresh lemon, quartered

1. Rinse chicken and pat dry. Discard giblets and neck or reserve for another use. In a large skillet, brown chicken pieces in oil over medium-high heat until golden, about 5 minutes per side. Remove chicken and keep warm.

2. Put onions, garlic, and parsley in a 5-quart or larger crockery slow-cooker. Arrange chicken on top of onions. Surround with potatoes, turnip, tomatoes, and green beans.

3. In a small bowl, combine stock, thyme, and rosemary. Pour over chicken. Scatter leeks over chicken. Drizzle chicken and vegetables with vinegar. Do not stir. Cover and cook on LOW for 6 to 8 hours or on HIGH for 2¼ to 2¾ hours.

4. Transfer chicken and vegetables to a large heated platter. Serve with lemon wedges. Pass any pan juices separately to spoon over each serving.

PREP TIME: 25 MIN

COOK TIME: 6–8 HR ON LOW OR 2¼–2¾ HR ON HIGH

Per serving: 402 calories, 42 g protein, 9 g total fat (1.9 g saturated), 38 g carbohydrates, 196 mg sodium, 115 mg cholesterol, 8 g dietary fiber

TEX-MEX CHICKEN

MAKES 6 SERVINGS

Tex-Mex is popular throughout the Heartland—it was probably introduced to the Midwest in the mid-1800s by the Mexican cooks who served chili, tortillas, and beans from the chuckwagons on the cattle drives out of Texas.

If your family prefers less spicy food, stuff the chicken breasts with diced green bell pepper instead of the sliced jalapeños. Serve this mouth-watering, piquant chicken on a bed of hot steamed rice and offer warmed tortillas to mop up the sauce.

6 boneless, skinless chicken breast halves (about 2 pounds total)
3 to 4 jalapeño chile peppers, seeded and thinly sliced
3 large garlic cloves, minced
6 slices bacon
1 teaspoon dried oregano leaves, crumbled
¼ teaspoon chili powder
¼ teaspoon ground cumin
Salt, optional, and freshly ground black pepper to taste

1 large yellow onion, chopped (1½ cups)
4 tomatillos, husked and chopped (1 cup)
1 medium red bell pepper, seeded and chopped (1 cup)
1 14½-ounce can whole tomatoes, undrained and chopped
¼ cup dry red wine
2 tablespoons tomato paste
½ cup drained pitted black olives
¼ cup chopped fresh cilantro for garnish

1. Rinse chicken and pat dry. Place each breast between 2 sheets of waxed paper or plastic wrap. Lightly pound with the flat side of a meat mallet to flatten evenly to about ½-inch thickness. Place 2 jalapeño slices (3 or 4 if you like a hotter chicken) and ½ teaspoon of the minced garlic in the center of each chicken piece. Fold in the sides, enclosing the pepper and garlic. Wrap each breast with a slice of bacon. Secure with a toothpick or short skewer. In a small bowl, mix together oregano, chili powder, cumin, salt, and pepper. Sprinkle on chicken.

PREP TIME: 25 MIN
COOK TIME: 6–8 HR ON LOW OR 2–2½ HR ON HIGH

2. Put onion, tomatillos, and bell pepper in a 3½-quart or larger crockery slow-cooker. Arrange chicken breasts on top of vegetables. In a medium bowl, combine tomatoes, wine, and tomato paste. Pour over chicken. Do not stir. Cover and cook on LOW for 6 to 8 hours or on HIGH for 2 to 2½ hours.

3. To serve, arrange chicken breasts on a heated serving platter. Stir olives into pan juices and spoon over chicken. Garnish with cilantro.

Per serving: 352 calories, 39 g protein, 16 g total fat (5.5 g saturated), 10 g carbohydrates, 474 mg sodium, 103 mg cholesterol, 2 g dietary fiber

ROASTED TURKEY BREAST STUFFED WITH HERBS

MAKES 8 SERVINGS

For more than forty years, the legendary Johnny Appleseed wandered the land, preaching the Bible and plant-
ing apple trees. According to the legend, many apple orchards in the Midwest, particularly in the states of
Illinois, Indiana, and Ohio, are a direct result of his efforts.

You have the making of a company dinner here. The slow-roasted turkey breast is stuffed with herbs and
napped with an apple-scented leek sauce. Serve this with whipped butternut squash and sautéed sugar snap peas.

If using a 3½- or 4-quart slow-cooker, use a 2- 2½-pound boneless turkey breast half.

1 4- to 5-pound boneless turkey breast with skin	4 medium leeks, white part, and 1 inch pale green, well rinsed and thinly sliced (4 cups)
½ cup chopped fresh flat-leaf parsley	3 tablespoons fresh lemon juice
1 tablespoon fresh thyme leaves or 1 teaspoon dried, crumbled	1 cup chicken stock (page 53) or canned low-sodium broth
1 tablespoon grated lemon rind	½ cup dry white wine
2 tart apples, such as Granny Smith, Ida Red, Prairie Spy, or Mutsu, peeled, cored, and chopped (2 cups)	2 tablespoons butter, at room temperature
	2 tablespoons unbleached all-purpose flour

PREP TIME:
20 MIN

COOK TIME:
8–10 HR ON LOW +
15 MIN ON HIGH OR
3³/₄–4¹/₄ HR ON HIGH
+ OPTIONAL 5 MIN
UNDER BROILER

STAND TIME:
10 MIN

1. Rinse turkey breast and pat dry. Lightly pound the breast and, using your fingers, gently separate turkey skin from breast meat. Combine parsley, thyme, and lemon rind. Rub turkey breast inside and under the skin with the herb mixture; replace skin and tie in place with kitchen string.

2. Arrange apples and leeks in bottom of a 5-quart or larger crockery slow-cooker. Top with turkey breast, skin side up. Drizzle lemon juice over turkey breast. Cover and cook on LOW for 8 to 10 hours or on HIGH for 3½ to 4 hours, until tender.

3. Transfer turkey breast to a heated serving platter and keep warm. (If browner skin is preferred, place turkey breast in a shallow roasting pan and brown under a preheated broiler for 5 minutes.) Let turkey breast stand for 10 minutes before carving.

4. Meanwhile, if cooking on LOW, change setting to HIGH. Whisk stock and wine into pan drippings in slow-cook-er. In a small bowl, combine butter and flour. Whisk into slow-cooker and cook, uncovered, stirring occasional-ly, until thickened and bubbly, about 15 minutes. Cook and stir for another minute. Pour sauce into a gravy boat to spoon over turkey breast slices.

Per serving: 406 calories, 49 g protein, 16 g total fat (5.6 g saturated), 11 g carbohydrates, 142 mg sodium, 127 mg cholesterol, 2 g dietary fiber

TURKEY LOAF WITH CRANBERRY GLAZE

MAKES 8 SERVINGS

My mother used to make this loaf with chicken that she put through the meat grinder, but you can buy ground turkey in most supermarkets.

Since some packaged ground turkey contains the skin, which adds lots of fat, be sure to check the label to determine the fat content (it should be about 7 percent). You can also purchase a turkey breast, have your butcher remove the skin, and grind it for you. Any leftovers make very fine sandwiches the next day.

TURKEY LOAF

- 2 pounds ground turkey
- 1 small yellow onion, minced (½ cup)
- 2 green onions, sliced, including some green tops (¼ cup)
- 1 small celery rib, minced (¼ cup)
- ½ small green bell pepper, seeded and minced (¼ cup)
- 1 large garlic clove, minced
- 2 large eggs, lightly beaten
- ⅓ cup fresh bread crumbs
- 2 tablespoons ketchup
  Salt, optional, and freshly ground black pepper to taste
- ⅛ teaspoon cayenne pepper

CRANBERRY GLAZE

- 1 16-ounce can whole-berry cranberry sauce
- ⅓ cup golden raisins
- 1 tablespoon fresh orange juice
- 1 teaspoon grated orange rind
- ⅛ teaspoon ground cinnamon
- ⅛ teaspoon ground cloves

PREP TIME: 20 MIN

COOK TIME: 8–9 HR ON LOW OR 3½–4¼ HR ON HIGH

STAND TIME: 20 MIN

1. In a large bowl, combine all turkey loaf ingredients. Mix thoroughly with your hands. Form into a 6-inch round loaf to fit a 3½-quart or larger crockery slow-cooker.

2. Place a metal rack or trivet in the slow-cooker and put turkey loaf on top of rack. Cover and cook on LOW for 8 to 9 hours or on HIGH for 3½ to 4¼ hours.

3. About 50 minutes before loaf is done, combine ingredients for glaze. Spoon glaze on top of turkey loaf. Cook, covered, until turkey loaf is done and glaze is hot.

4. Transfer turkey loaf to a heated serving platter. Let stand for 20 minutes before slicing and serving. Spoon any pan juices over top.

Per serving: 267 calories, 30 g protein, 3 g total fat (0.8 g saturated), 31 g carbohydrates, 142 mg sodium, 130 mg cholesterol, 1 g dietary fiber

TURKEY BREAST WITH OKRA AND TOMATOES

MAKES 6 SERVINGS

This is the kind of dish to prepare when the tomatoes are full of sun-warmed taste and the okra in the garden is still finger-length, firm, and bright green.

If your market doesn't sell turkey breast halves, ask your butcher to cut a whole fresh turkey breast for you, wrapping the second half for the freezer to roast later.

Serve this savory dish with corn bread or spooned over mashed potatoes.

2   medium yellow onions, thinly sliced (3 cups)
2   medium celery ribs, thinly sliced (1 cup)
2   large garlic cloves, minced
1   tablespoon olive oil
1   teaspoon turmeric
1   2½- to 3-pound boneless, skinless turkey breast half

6   plum tomatoes, cut in half lengthwise
2   teaspoons chopped fresh thyme leaves or ½ teaspoon dried, crumbled
½   cup water
1   pound fresh okra, stem ends trimmed

PREP TIME: 20 MIN

COOK TIME: 6–7 HR ON LOW OR 2½–3 HR ON HIGH

1. In a large skillet, brown onions, celery, and garlic in olive oil over medium heat until onions are limp, about 5 minutes. Sprinkle on turmeric.

2. While onions are browning, rinse turkey breast and pat dry. Cut turkey into 2-inch chunks.

Transfer onion mixture to a 3½-quart or larger crockery slow-cooker. In same skillet, brown turkey pieces over medium heat for 5 minutes, turning occasionally to brown all sides. Arrange turkey pieces on top of onions. Arrange tomatoes, cut side down, around turkey. Add thyme and water. Do not stir. Cover and cook on LOW for 5½ to 6½ hours or on HIGH for 2¼ to 2¾ hours.

3. Add the okra. Continue to cook, covered, until okra is tender, about 30 minutes if cooking on LOW or 15 minutes if cooking on HIGH.

4. To serve, transfer turkey and vegetables to a heated serving platter. Stir pan juices and spoon over turkey.

Per serving: 306 calories, 52 g protein, 5 g total fat (1.0 g saturated), 13 g carbohydrates, 114 mg sodium, 141 mg cholesterol, 3 g dietary fiber

CREAMY BAKED GAME HENS WITH TARRAGON

MAKES 2 SERVINGS

Cornish game hens, an American hybrid of a Plymouth Rock hen and a Cornish rooster, have become quite popular in the Midwest. You'll find them fresh or frozen in most every supermarket.

This easy-to-fix game hen dish makes a lovely intimate supper for two when a special occasion falls midweek and you're at work or away all day. Serve it with orzo and steamed broccoli topped with buttered crumbs. Orzo, a tiny rice-shaped pasta, is available in larger supermarkets, Italian markets, and specialty food shops. If it's not available, substitute rice.

½ pound small white boiling onions
Water
2 1¼- to 1½-pound Cornish game hens
Salt, optional, and freshly ground black pepper to taste
1 tablespoon olive oil

2 tablespoon chopped fresh tarragon leaves or 2 teaspoons dried, crumbled
½ cup chicken stock (page 53) or canned low-sodium broth
2 tablespoons brandy, optional
⅓ cup heavy cream

PREP TIME: 25 MIN

COOK TIME: 7–9 HR ON LOW + 15 MIN ON HIGH OR 3¼–3¾ HR ON HIGH

1. Using a sharp knife, make a small X in the root end of each onion. Bring a saucepan of water to a boil. Add the onions, lower the heat, and simmer for 5 minutes. Drain and rinse under running cold water. Slip skins off onions.

2. Meanwhile, rinse hens and pat dry. Discard giblets and necks or reserve for another use. Season inside and out with salt and pepper. Tie legs together with kitchen string. Heat oil in a large skillet over medium-high heat. Add hens and brown on all sides, about 10 minutes.

3. Put hens in a 3½-quart or larger crockery slow-cooker (if using a 3½- or 4-quart slow-cooker, the hens will need to stand on end, neck end down; in larger slow-cookers, they can set side by side). Surround with onions. Sprinkle with half of the tarragon. Pour on stock. Cover and cook on LOW for 7 to 9 hours or on HIGH for 3 to 3½ hours.

4. Transfer hens and onions to a heated serving platter; remove kitchen strings and keep warm. If cooking on LOW, change setting to HIGH. Stir pan juices and skim off any surface fat. Stir in brandy if desired. Cook, uncovered, for 5 minutes. Add cream and cook, uncovered, until slightly thickened, about 10 minutes. Pour sauce over hens and sprinkle with remaining chopped tarragon.

Per serving: 1011 calories, 87 g protein, 63 g total fat (21.7 g saturated), 12 g carbohydrates, 157 mg sodium, 322 mg cholesterol, 2 g dietary fiber

FRUIT-STUFFED GAME HENS

MAKES 4 SERVINGS

This is a lovely dish. The cranberries give the stuffing a slightly tart flavor that nicely complements the richness of the hens.

Dried cranberries are available in larger supermarkets, natural foods stores, and specialty food shops and by mail order (see Sources, page 142). Serve this with steamed kale or escarole dressed with lemon and garlic and wedges of baked winter squash.

If using a 3½- or 4-quart slow-cooker, prepare half of the recipe.

4   1¼- to 1½-pound Cornish game hens
    Salt, optional, and freshly ground
    black pepper to taste
               STUFFING
⅓   cup dried cranberries
6   dried apricots, finely chopped (¼ cup)
4   dried apples, finely chopped (¼ cup)
¼   cup dried currants
1   small yellow onion, chopped (½ cup)
1   medium celery rib with leaves, chopped
    (¾ cup)

2   tablespoons butter, melted
1   tablespoon chopped fresh sage leaves
    or 1 teaspoon dried, crumbled
    Salt, optional, and freshly ground
    black pepper to taste
¼   cup fresh bread crumbs
¼   cup dry white wine
1   large lemon, cut in half

**PREP TIME:
20 MIN**

**COOK TIME:
6–8 HR ON LOW OR
2 ³/₄–3 ¹/₂ HR ON HIGH
+ OPTIONAL
5 MIN UNDER
BROILER**

1. Rinse hens inside and out and pat dry. Discard giblets and necks or reserve for another use. Sprinkle cavities with salt and pepper.

2. In a large bowl, combine dried fruits, onion, celery, melted butter, sage, salt, and pepper. Stir in bread crumbs. Moisten with wine. Evenly divide stuffing mixture among the hens, filling the large cavity only. Cross hen legs to secure stuffing and tie with kitchen string. Rub the skin of each hen with the cut lemon.

3. Place a wire rack or metal trivet in the bottom of a 5-quart or larger crockery slow-cooker. Put hens on end, neck end down, on top of rack. (Do not add any liquid.) Cover and cook on LOW for 6 to 8 hours or on HIGH for 2¾ to 3½ hours. To serve, remove kitchen string from hens.

4. If desired, transfer hens to a baking sheet or a heat-proof platter and brown under a preheated broiler until golden brown, about 5 minutes. Serve with any pan juices spooned over the top.

Per serving: 897 calories, 84 g protein, 48 g total fat (15.2 g saturated), 27 g carbohydrates, 210 mg sodium, 283 mg cholesterol, 3 g dietary fiber

ROASTED DUCK WITH CRANBERRY SAUCE

MAKES 4 SERVINGS

Wisconsin is cranberry and duck country—fortuitously, the two make a delightful flavor combination. Since fresh cranberries have such a short season, it's a good idea to freeze a bag or two so you can enjoy this dish year-round, or use dried cranberries. To keep dried cranberries from molding, store them in the refrigerator or freezer.

If using a 3½- or 4-quart slow-cooker, prepare a duckling half, cut into quarters.

1 4- to 5-pound ready-to-cook duckling	1 tablespoon butter, melted
Salt, optional, and freshly ground black pepper to taste	1 tablespoon fresh lemon juice
4 medium carrots, peeled and quartered	1 tablespoon Worcestershire sauce
4 medium celery ribs, quartered	¼ cup ruby port or 1½ tablespoons balsamic vinegar
1 large yellow onion, peeled and cut into eighths	2 cups chicken stock (page 53) or canned low-sodium broth
6 large garlic cloves	1 cup fresh cranberries, rinsed, or ⅓ cup dried
4 sprigs fresh thyme or 1 teaspoon dried leaves, crumbled	
4 sprigs fresh flat-leaf parsley	

PREP TIME: 15 MIN

COOK TIME: 6–7 HR ON LOW or 3–3½ HR ON HIGH + 15–20 MIN IN OVEN FOR BROWNING

STAND TIME: 15 MIN

1. Rinse duckling inside and out and pat dry. Discard giblets, neck, and any lumps of duck fat or reserve for another use. With a fork, prick skin all over at 2-inch intervals. Place a metal rack or trivet in bottom of a 5-quart or larger crockery slow-cooker. Season duckling body cavity with salt and pepper. Fill cavity with carrots, celery, onion, garlic, thyme, and parsley. Set duckling, breast side up, on top of rack.

2. In a small bowl, combine butter, lemon juice, and Worcestershire sauce. Brush over duckling. Cover and cook on LOW for 6 to 7 hours or on HIGH for 3 to 3½ hours, until meat near thigh bone is very tender when pierced. If possible, remove excess fat twice during cooking time.

3. A half hour before serving, preheat oven to 400°F. Transfer duckling to a shallow roasting pan and brown in oven for 15 to 20 minutes. Remove duckling from oven and let stand for 15 minutes before carving.

4. Meanwhile, if cooking on LOW, change setting to HIGH. Remove excess fat from pan drippings. Stir in port and deglaze slow-cooker by stirring to loosen any browned particles. Stir in stock and cranberries. Cook, uncovered, stirring occasionally, until reduced by half, about 10 minutes.

5. Carve duckling into serving pieces, spooning some of the cranberry sauce over each serving. Pour remainder into a gravy boat to serve on the side.

Per serving: 819 calories, 43 g protein, 62 g total fat (21.9 g saturated), 18 g carbohydrates, 292 mg sodium, 181 mg cholesterol, 4 g dietary fiber

BRAISED PHEASANT WITH KUMQUATS

MAKES 4 SERVINGS

Pheasant are plentiful game birds on my family's Kansas farms. Each fall my father used to host several hunting parties in search of the delicious birds. The flesh of wild pheasant is red and has a gamier flavor than the commercially raised pheasants available in specialty meat markets. Allowed a diet of corn and nuts, farm-raised pheasant tastes something like chicken.

My market sells kumquats from November through May. At other times of the year, substitute a sliced, unpeeled thin-skinned orange, such as Valencia, and cut each slice into quarters.

If using a 3½- or 4-quart slow-cooker, cut the pheasant into serving pieces before cooking.

1 pheasant (about 2¾ pounds)
1 tablespoon olive oil
  Salt, optional, and freshly ground black pepper to taste
4 sprigs fresh flat-leaf parsley
2 large garlic cloves, peeled
1 large bay leaf
3 slices bacon
1 medium yellow onion, chopped (1 cup)
1 medium carrot, peeled and chopped (¾ cup)
1½ cups chicken stock (page 53) or canned low-sodium broth

2 tablespoons brandy, optional
1 teaspoon chopped fresh thyme leaves or ¼ teaspoon dried, crumbled
8 kumquats, scrubbed and sliced, large seeds removed
1 cup water
2 tablespoons sugar
2 tablespoons balsamic vinegar
2 tablespoons cornstarch dissolved in 2 tablespoons cold water

PREP TIME:
20 MIN

COOK TIME:
6–8 HR ON LOW +
45 MIN ON HIGH
OR 2¾–3½ HR
ON HIGH

1. Rinse pheasant, cleaning the cavity well, and pat dry. Discard giblets and neck or reserve for another use. Rub outside of pheasant with olive oil. Season cavity with salt and pepper. Stuff with parsley, garlic, and bay leaf.

2. Place a metal rack or trivet in the bottom of a 5-quart or larger crockery slow-cooker. Set pheasant, breast side up, on rack. Arrange bacon slices lengthwise across pheasant, starting at the neck and ending at the tail. Surround pheasant with onion and carrot. Pour ¼ cup stock into slow-cooker. Cover and cook on LOW for 6 to 8 hours or on HIGH for 2 to 2¾ hours, until juices run clear when thigh is pierced with the tip of a knife. Transfer pheasant to a heated platter and keep warm. Discard parsley, garlic, and bay leaf.

3. Skim excess fat from pan juices. If cooking on LOW, change setting to HIGH. Stir brandy and thyme leaves into pan juices. Add kumquats, water, and sugar. Stir and cook until kumquats are translucent, about 15 minutes. Using a slotted spoon, remove kumquats and reserve. Stir remaining 1¼ cups stock into slow-cooker. Cook, uncovered, stirring occasionally, until sauce is reduced by half, about 15 minutes. Whisk together vinegar and cornstarch. Stir into reduced sauce and continue to cook uncovered, stirring, until sauce is thickened, about 15 minutes. Stir in reserved kumquats.

4. Carve pheasant, pouring some of the sauce over each serving. Pass any remaining sauce separately.

Per serving: 607 calories, 50 g protein, 32 g total fat (9.7 g saturated), 23 g carbohydrates, 236 mg sodium, 154 mg cholesterol, 4 g dietary fiber

PHEASANT WITH PEACHES

MAKES 4 SERVINGS

Nowadays one can buy good-quality peaches year-round. The sweetness of the peach and the heat of the chile pepper complement the flavor of the pheasant. ▶

PHEASANT WITH PEACHES *(see previous page for photo and notes)*

1 pheasant (about 2¾ pounds), quartered
Ground cumin to taste
Salt, optional, and freshly ground
black pepper to taste
1 tablespoon olive oil
1 Anaheim chile pepper, seeded and minced
(¼ cup)

2 large garlic cloves, minced
4 slices bacon, cut in half
1½ cups chicken stock (page 53) or canned
low-sodium broth
2 large ripe peaches

PREP TIME:
15 MIN

COOK TIME:
6–8 HR ON LOW +
5 MIN ON HIGH
OR 2½–3 HR
ON HIGH

1. Rinse pheasant and pat dry. Discard giblets and neck or reserve for another use. Season with cumin, salt, and black pepper. In a large skillet, brown pheasant pieces in olive oil over medium-high heat, about 5 minutes per side.

2. Transfer pheasant to a 3½-quart or larger crockery slow-cooker. Scatter chile and garlic over pheasant. Place 2 bacon half-slices on each quarter, making an X. Pour in ½ cup stock; do not stir. Cover, and cook on LOW for 6 to 8 hours or on HIGH for 2¼ to 2¾ hours.

3. Transfer pheasant quarters to a heated serving platter. Keep warm.

4. If cooking on LOW, change setting to HIGH. Skim off surface fat and stir pan juices. Peel, halve, and pit the peaches. Cut each peach half into 8 slices. Add to slow-cooker along with remaining stock. Cook, uncovered, until peaches are heated through and slightly cooked, about 5 minutes. Spoon sauce and peaches over pheasant.

Per serving: 434 calories, 46 g protein, 23 g total fat (7.6 g saturated), 8 g carbohydrates, 248 mg sodium, 132 mg cholesterol, 1 g dietary fiber

RABBIT WITH SPRING VEGETABLES

MAKES 4 SERVINGS

Low in fat and cholesterol, rabbit is a favorite dish among the Italians and Eastern Europeans who settled in the Heartland. If fresh domestic rabbit is available, by all means use it, or ask your supermarket to order a good-quality frozen rabbit. This recipe works quite well with cut-up chicken if you can't find rabbit.

Serve this dish in a wide, shallow soup bowl along with some crusty bread and a salad of romaine and butterhead lettuces, tossed with walnut oil and raspberry vinegar and topped with toasted walnuts and strips of Gruyère cheese.

1 3-pound rabbit, cut into serving pieces
1 small yellow onion, chopped (½ cup)
1 medium celery rib, chopped (½ cup)
1 small carrot, peeled and chopped (½ cup)
8 small carrots, peeled
4 large garlic cloves, peeled
4 small turnips, peeled
4 small white onions, peeled
2 medium leeks, white part only, well rinsed and chopped (1 cup)

8 medium button mushrooms
1 large bay leaf
1 tablespoon chopped fresh flat-leaf parsley
1 teaspoon fresh thyme leaves or ¼ teaspoon dried, crumbled
1 quart chicken stock (page 53) or canned low-sodium broth
   Salt, optional, and freshly ground black pepper to taste

PREP TIME: 25 MIN

COOK TIME: 8–10 HR ON LOW + 15 MIN ON HIGH OR 3–4 HR ON HIGH

1. Rinse rabbit well and pat dry. Arrange chopped onion, celery, and carrot in a 3½-quart or larger crockery slow-cooker. Place rabbit pieces on top of vegetables.
2. Put whole vegetables on top and around the rabbit pieces. Add bay leaf, parsley, and thyme. Pour stock over all. Do not stir. Cover and cook on LOW for 8 to 10 hours or on HIGH for 2¾ to 3¾ hours.
3. To serve, arrange rabbit pieces in 4 wide, shallow soup bowls, dividing the vegetables among the servings. Keep warm. If cooking on LOW, change setting to HIGH and cook, uncovered, until pan juices are reduced by one-third, about 15 minutes. Season with salt and pepper; discard bay leaf. Ladle some of the sauce over each serving.

Per serving: 562 calories, 66 g protein, 18 g total fat (5.2 g saturated), 32 g carbohydrates, 295 mg sodium, 161 mg cholesterol, 8 g dietary fiber

MEATS

A S YOU MIGHT EXPECT, MEAT IS popular in the Midwest, where it's not unusual to eat meat at every meal, including breakfast. Excellent beef is plentiful, and your crockery slow-cooker will help you prepare the most succulent beef dishes you've ever cooked.

The Midwest, particularly Iowa, is pork country. In a slow-cooker, pork will become meltingly tender and juicy. Lamb is becoming increasingly popular in the Midwest, and today lamb farms abound in Indiana and Minnesota. You'll also find recipes for luscious veal dishes and a delicious way to slow-roast buffalo, the "new meat" now being grown by enterprising Midwestern ranchers.

This collection of mouth-watering recipes is the kind of simple, hearty, farm-style food that's equally appropriate for family or guests. Some of the recipes will bring back special childhood memories of snowbound Sunday suppers. Many turn less costly cuts of meat into unsurpassed dishes that are meltingly tender, moist, and delicious. Others reflect the many ethnic influences on today's Heartland cooking. All are full of luscious, aromatic flavors that come from the long simmering of your crockery slow-cooker. And, if you happen to have any leftovers, you'll find that the dishes are even better reheated the next day.

BEEF STOCK

MAKES 3 QUARTS NON-REDUCED STOCK

PREP TIME: 15 MIN + 1 HR FOR ROASTING VEGETABLES IN OVEN

COOK TIME 10–12 HR ON LOW • OR 5-6 HR ON HIGH

Ask your butcher to crack the bones for your beef stock. For an even richer flavor, boil the strained stock on top of the stove until it reduces by half. The bones and vegetables are pre-roasted in the oven for 1 hour to intensify the flavor of the stock, so plan accordingly. This is a good project for a day when you plan to stay at home. If using a 3½- or 4-quart slow-cooker, prepare half of the recipe.

2½ pounds beef and veal bones
(marrow, knuckle, and shin)
1 large yellow onion, peeled and cut in half
1 large carrot, peeled and quartered
1 large celery rib with leaves, quartered
1 leek, white part only, well rinsed and quartered

2 large garlic cloves, peeled
3 sprigs fresh flat-leaf parsley
2 sprigs fresh thyme
3 black peppercorns or to taste
3 quarts water

1. Preheat oven to 400°F. Put bones in a single layer in a large roasting pan. Scatter vegetables, herbs, and peppercorns among the bones. Roast uncovered for 1 hour.

2. Transfer bones and vegetables to a 5-quart or larger crockery slow-cooker. Add water, cover, and cook on LOW for 10 to 12 hours or on HIGH for 5 to 6 hours.

3. Strain stock through a fine sieve or a colander lined with cheesecloth. Discard solids. If desired, cook stock in an uncovered saucepan on the top of the stove over high heat until reduced by half. Transfer stock to a covered container and refrigerate for several hours. Skim off any fat that rises to the top. Refrigerate, covered tightly, for up to 3 days or freeze for up to 3 months.

Per 1-cup serving: 24 calories, 1 g protein, trace total fat (trace saturated), 5 g carbohydrates, 32 mg sodium, 0 cholesterol, 1 g dietary fiber

BEEF STROGANOFF

MAKES 4 SERVINGS

Years ago the actor Robert Young and I were both guests on a television cooking show. Afterward Mr. Young, a native of Chicago, gave me his recipe for Beef Stroganoff, which I've adapted here for the crockery slow-cooker. Serve it over buttered noodles or with a pilaf made from barley or quinoa, an ancient Incan grain now grown in Colorado that is rapidly gaining in popularity and availability throughout the Heartland.

1½ pounds boneless top round beef steak, trimmed of fat
Salt, optional, and freshly ground black pepper to taste
1 tablespoon mild vegetable oil, such as canola
2 medium yellow onions, sliced and separated into rings (3 cups)
¾ pound button mushrooms, sliced (3¾ cups)
1 tablespoon sweet paprika

¼ cup cognac or brandy, optional
1½ cups beef stock (page 82) or canned low-sodium broth
½ tablespoon Dijon-style mustard
½ tablespoon Worcestershire sauce
1 cup heavy cream
2 tablespoons unbleached all-purpose flour
¼ teaspoon freshly grated nutmeg
Fresh flat-leaf parsley, chopped, for garnish

PREP TIME: 25 MIN

COOK TIME: 7–8 HR ON LOW + 30 MIN ON HIGH OR 4–4½ HR ON HIGH

1. Cut beef across grain into ¼-inch slanting slices (the meat will be easier to slice if you chill the beef in the freezer for about 30 minutes first). Season beef with salt and pepper.

2. In a large skillet, heat oil over medium-high heat. Add half of the beef and brown on all sides, about 5 minutes. Using a slotted spoon, transfer browned beef to a 3½-quart or larger crockery slow-cooker. Repeat process, browning remaining beef and transferring it to slow-cooker.

3. Arrange onions and mushrooms on top of beef. Sprinkle with paprika. Combine cognac, stock, mustard, and Worcestershire sauce. Pour over all. Do not stir. Cover and cook on LOW for 7 to 8 hours or on HIGH for 3½ to 4 hours.

4. If cooking on LOW, change setting to HIGH. In a medium bowl, whisk together cream, flour, and nutmeg. Whisk in ½ cup of the hot cooking liquid. Add mixture to slow-cooker; stir gently. Cook, covered, until hot and thickened, about 30 minutes. Transfer to a serving platter lined with cooked noodles or a pilaf, and garnish with parsley.

Per serving: 575 calories, 46 g protein, 33 g total fat (16.4 g saturated), 15 g carbohydrates, 200 mg sodium, 187 mg cholesterol, 3 g dietary fiber

BEER-BRAISED BRISKET

MAKES 4 SERVINGS

Midwesterners love to cook with beer, especially in Missouri and Wisconsin, the beer capitals of the United States. Brisket is usually sold in halves. Use the pointed front cut for this full-flavored dish. It's more economical, and the long slow-cooking brings out its rich flavor. The dried fruits add a delightful flavor surprise. Serve this dish some snow-bound evening in wide shallow soup bowls with plenty of crusty bread for mopping up the sauce.

2 large garlic cloves, minced	2 medium yellow onions, chopped (2 cups)
1 tablespoon Worcestershire sauce	3 plum tomatoes, sliced (1 cup)
1 tablespoon minced fresh thyme leaves or 1 teaspoon dried, crumbled	1 cup raisins
1 teaspoon minced fresh marjoram leaves or ¼ teaspoon dried, crumbled	10 dried figs, split in half lengthwise
Salt, optional, and freshly ground black pepper to taste	1½ cups beer
1 2- to 2½-pound beef brisket, well trimmed of excess fat	½ pound button mushrooms, trimmed and quartered

PREP TIME: 10 MIN

COOK TIME: 8–10 HR ON LOW OR 4–5 HR ON HIGH

1. In a small bowl, combine garlic, Worcestershire sauce, thyme, marjoram, salt, and pepper. Rub over both sides of the brisket.

2. Put onions in a 3½-quart or larger crockery slow-cooker. Top with tomatoes and the brisket. If necessary, cut brisket to fit. Scatter raisins and figs around edges. Pour in beer. Do not stir. Cover and cook on LOW for 7½ to 9½ hours or on HIGH for 3¾ to 4¾ hours.

3. Add mushrooms and cook, covered, until mushrooms are just tender and heated through, about 30 minutes if cooking on LOW or 15 minutes if cooking on HIGH.

4. To serve, carve brisket into thin slices. Arrange beef, vegetables, and fruits in wide, shallow soup bowls. Spoon on pan juices.

Per serving: 725 calories, 58 g protein, 20 g total fat (9 g saturated), 266 g carbohydrates, 77 mg sodium, 158 mg cholesterol, 8 g dietary fiber

BUFFALO ROAST WITH MUSTARD GLAZE

MAKES 8 SERVINGS

Similar in flavor to beef but with only half the calories, buffalo is now being ranch-raised in several Midwestern states. Since it's very lean, it will benefit from simmering in a crockery slow-cooker (this recipe doesn't work well on high). You'll need to marinate the meat for a day before it's cooked, so plan accordingly.

If your meat market doesn't carry buffalo, ask your butcher to special order it or you can order it by mail (see Sources, page 142).

1 3-pound boneless buffalo rump roast, rolled and tied
⅓ cup fresh orange juice (1 small orange)
¼ cup Dijon-style mustard
2 tablespoons honey

2 tablespoons soy sauce
4 large shallots, minced (¼ cup)
1 small jalapeño chile pepper, minced
½ pound seedless red grapes, cut in half (1½ cups)

1. Put buffalo roast in a glass ceramic dish. Whisk together remaining ingredients except grapes and pour over roast. Cover tightly with plastic wrap and refrigerate for 24 hours, turning meat occasionally.

2. Transfer buffalo roast and marinade to a 3½-quart or larger crockery slow-cooker. If necessary, cut roast to fit. Cover and cook on LOW for 8 to 10 hours.

3. Transfer roast to a heated platter and let stand for 10 to 15 minutes before carving crosswise into thin slices.

4. Meanwhile, stir pan juices and add grapes. Cook, covered, until grapes are heated through, about 10 minutes. Pour sauce into a gravy boat to spoon over each serving.

PREP TIME:
15 MIN + 24 HR
FOR MARINATING

COOK TIME:
8–10 HR ON LOW +
10 MIN FOR MAKING
SAUCE

STAND TIME:
10–15 MIN

Per serving: 243 calories, 38 g protein, 4 g total fat (1.3 g saturated), 13 g carbohydrates, 521 mg sodium, 105 mg cholesterol, trace dietary fiber

CHICKEN FRIED STEAK WITH BLACK PEPPER GRAVY

MAKES 6 SERVINGS

This is a dish that I could happily eat often. Made in the crockery slow-cooker, the meat is exceptionally moist, fork-tender, and flavorful—nothing like the tough, thickly battered steak so often served today. The slow-cooking eliminates the need to pound the steak before cooking, a must when preparing on top of the stove.
Serve this family dinner with garlic mashed potatoes and a salad of mixed greens with a creamy dressing.

½ cup unbleached all-purpose flour
1 teaspoon sweet paprika
¼ teaspoon dried basil leaves, crumbled
¼ teaspoon dried thyme leaves, crumbled
⅛ teaspoon garlic powder
⅛ teaspoon onion powder
　Salt, optional, and freshly ground
　black pepper to taste
1½ pounds boneless beef round steak,
　cut ¾ inch thick

2 tablespoons mild vegetable oil, such as canola
1½ cups beef stock (page 82) or canned
　low-sodium broth

BLACK PEPPER GRAVY

5 tablespoons unbleached all-purpose flour
3½ cups whole milk
½ teaspoon freshly ground black pepper
　Salt, optional

**PREP TIME:
15 MIN**

**COOK TIME:
8–10 HR ON LOW OR
4–5 HR ON HIGH +
15 MIN ON STOVE
FOR MAKING
GRAVY**

1. In a small bowl, combine the ½ cup flour, paprika, basil, thyme, garlic powder, onion powder, salt, and pepper. Cut steak into 6 serving pieces. Dredge steak pieces with seasoned flour, pressing as much flour as possible into the steak pieces. Reserve any leftover seasoned flour.
2. In a large skillet, heat oil over medium-high heat. Add steak pieces and brown, about 5 minutes per side.
3. Transfer browned steak to a 3½-quart or larger crockery slow-cooker; pour in stock. Cover and cook on LOW for 8 to 10 hours or on HIGH for 4 to 5 hours. If cooking on HIGH, stir once during last half hour of cooking. Transfer steak to a heated serving platter. Keep warm.
4. To make Black Pepper Gravy: Transfer pan juices to a large skillet. Over medium heat on top of the stove, whisk in the 5 tablespoons flour plus any reserved seasoned flour. Cook until golden brown, whisking continuously. Gradually stir in milk and continue to cook, whisking constantly, until thickened. Stir in pepper and season with salt to taste. Pour gravy into a gravy boat to serve with steaks.

Per serving: 403 calories, 30 g protein, 22 g total fat (8.0 g saturated), 20 g carbohydrates, 138 mg sodium, 80 mg cholesterol, 1 g dietary fiber

DRY-RUBBED BARBECUE BEEF BRISKET

MAKES 6 SERVINGS

Kansas City cooks are known for their barbecued beef. The secret is in a dry rub of spices. Traditionally the sauce is added at the very end or served on the side. I've adapted a recipe that I clipped years ago from the Kansas City Star *so that it works in a crockery slow-cooker.*

This beef is terrific for sandwiches, tucked into toasted kaiser rolls.

DRY RUB

- 1 teaspoon chili powder
- 1 teaspoon light brown sugar
- ½ teaspoon garlic powder
- ½ teaspoon paprika
- ¼ teaspoon lemon pepper seasoning
- ¼ teaspoon dry mustard
- ¼ teaspoon onion powder
- ¼ teaspoon dried thyme leaves, crumbled
- ⅛ teaspoon ground ginger

- 1 3-pound beef brisket, well trimmed of excess fat
- ½ cup water
- ½ teaspoon liquid smoke

BARBECUE SAUCE

- 1 cup ketchup
- 1 small yellow onion, minced (½ cup)
- 2 large garlic cloves, minced
- 2 tablespoons light brown sugar
- 2 tablespoons cider vinegar
- 2 tablespoons Worcestershire sauce
- ½ tablespoon dry mustard
- 1 teaspoon chili powder
- 1 teaspoon prepared horseradish
- ¼ teaspoon freshly ground black pepper
- ¼ teaspoon dried thyme leaves, crumbled
- ⅛ teaspoon dried rosemary leaves, crumbled

**PREP TIME:
30 MIN**

**COOK TIME:
8–10 HR ON LOW
OR 4–5 HR ON HIGH +
30 MIN ON LOW FOR
SIMMERING SAUCE**

**STAND TIME:
20 MIN**

1. In a small bowl, combine dry rub ingredients. Rub into both sides of brisket.
2. Place a wire rack or metal trivet in a 3½-quart or larger crockery slow-cooker. Combine water and liquid smoke. Pour into slow-cooker. Place brisket on wire rack. If necessary, cut brisket into 2 pieces to fit. Cover and cook on LOW for 7½ to 9½ hours or on HIGH for 4 to 5 hours.
3. About 1 hour before serving, combine barbecue sauce ingredients in a medium saucepan. Place over medium heat, bring to a simmer, and cook, stirring occasionally, for 30 minutes.
4. Lift brisket from slow-cooker and let stand for 20 minutes. Using tongs, remove metal rack and pour any pan liquids into barbecue sauce. If cooking on HIGH, change setting to LOW. Slice brisket very thin or shred. Return brisket to slow-cooker and cover with sauce. Stir well to combine. Cover the slow-cooker and cook for 30 minutes.
5. Transfer meat and sauce to a heated serving platter and serve.

Per serving: 428 calories, 48 g protein, 17 g total fat (6.0 g saturated), 19 g carbohydrates, 753 mg sodium, 141 mg cholesterol, 1 g dietary fiber

MIDWESTERN BOILED DINNER

MAKES 4 SERVINGS

Boiled dinner is an example of good Midwestern boardinghouse food where 20 or 30 pounds of meat are simmered at the back of the stove for hours awaiting dinnertime. Tender, wholesome, and satisfying, it's comfort in a soup plate. All of the ingredients are readily available year-round, but be sure to use top-quality meat and vegetables.

This recipe brings back fond childhood memories. Serve it with a horseradish cream sauce, a simple combination of sour cream or whipped heavy cream and prepared horseradish to taste.

4 lean beef short ribs (about 3 pounds total)
1 tablespoon olive oil
2 medium carrots, peeled and quartered
2 small turnips, trimmed and peeled
1 medium fennel bulb, trimmed and quartered
2 celery ribs, quartered
2 medium leeks pale-green, with 1 inch tops, well rinsed and cut in half lengthwise (2½ cups)
1 large yellow onion, peeled and cut into eighths
2 medium russet potatoes, peeled and quartered

2 large garlic cloves, peeled and halved
4 sprigs fresh thyme leaves or 1 teaspoon dried, crumbled
2 sprigs fresh flat-leaf parsley
1 large bay leaf
 Salt, optional, and freshly ground black pepper to taste
1 quart beef stock (page 82) or canned low-sodium broth
1 small cabbage (about ½ pound), cored and quartered

PREP TIME: 30 MIN

COOK TIME: 8½–9½ HR ON LOW OR 4¼–4¾ HR ON HIGH

1. In a large skillet, brown short ribs in oil over medium-high heat, turning to brown all sides. Transfer ribs to a 4-quart or larger crockery slow-cooker. Surround with the vegetables and herbs, except the cabbage, layering the ingredients in the order given. Season with salt and pepper. Add stock. Do not stir.

2. Cover and cook on LOW for 8 to 9 hours or on HIGH for 4 to 4½ hours. Add cabbage and cook, covered, for 30 minutes more if cooking on LOW or 15 minutes more if cooking on HIGH.

3. To serve, divide ribs among 4 shallow soup plates. Discard bay leaf. Top with vegetables and some of the pan juices.

Per serving: 493 calories, 37 g protein, 22 g total fat (7.8 g saturated), 39 g carbohydrate, 249 mg sodium, 82 mg cholesterol, 9 g dietary fiber

MOTHER'S MEAT LOAF

MAKES 8 SERVINGS

When I was growing up in Kansas, Saturday night usually meant meat loaf for dinner. I'm always trying new recipes for this slice of my past but keep coming back to the realization that my mother's was best. The recipe makes a big loaf, so there's plenty for sandwiches the next day.

2 pounds lean ground beef	Salt, optional, and freshly ground
½ pound ground pork	black pepper to taste
½ pound ground veal	2 large eggs, slightly beaten
1 large yellow onion, minced (1½ cups)	30 saltine crackers, finely crushed (1 cup)
1 small red bell pepper, seeded and minced (½ cup)	⅔ cup ketchup
1 large celery rib, minced (1 cup)	2 tablespoons light brown sugar
2 large garlic cloves, minced	½ teaspoon dry mustard
½ teaspoon dried thyme leaves, crumbled	½ teaspoon Worcestershire sauce
	⅛ teaspoon cayenne pepper

1. In a large bowl, combine ground beef, pork, veal, onion, bell pepper, celery, garlic, thyme, salt, and pepper. Add eggs, cracker crumbs, and ⅓ cup of the ketchup. Using your hands, gently mix and form into a thick round loaf, about 7 inches in diameter.

2. Place a wire rack or metal trivet in a 3½-quart or larger crockery slow-cooker. Place meat loaf on a double thickness of cheesecloth (about 24 inches square). Holding the edges of the cheesecloth, lower meat loaf into slow-cooker and position on top of wire rack. Fold cheesecloth loosely over top of meat loaf. Cover slow-cooker and cook on LOW for 7 to 9 hours or on HIGH for 3½ to 4 ½ hours.

3. During last 30 minutes of cooking time, in a small bowl, combine remaining ⅓ cup ketchup, brown sugar, dry mustard, Worcestershire sauce, and cayenne pepper. Spread over loaf. Cook, covered, until done.

4. Holding the edges of the cheesecloth, lift meat loaf from slow-cooker and place it on a heated serving platter. Remove and discard cheesecloth. Let meat loaf stand for 10 to 15 minutes before thinly slicing.

**PREP TIME:
20 MIN
COOK TIME:
7–9 HR ON LOW OR
3½–4½ HR ON HIGH
STAND TIME:
10–15 MIN**

Per serving: 417 calories, 37 g protein, 21 g total fat (7.7 g saturated), 19 g carbohydrates, 535 mg sodium, 138 mg cholesterol, 1 g dietary fiber

POT ROAST
SMOTHERED IN ONIONS

MAKES 6 SERVINGS

Each spring my dad would plant at least 100 onion sets in his garden. Like most Midwesterners, he loved onions and wanted plenty for my mother's cooking, such as this smothered pot roast, adapted for the crockery slow-cooker. The layer of apples cooked under the roast is unexpected and makes the dish quite delicious.

4 large cooking apples, such as Granny Smith, Northern Spy, or Rhode Island Greening, unpeeled, cored, and sliced ¼ inch thick
1 teaspoon ground cinnamon
1 2- to 2½-pound boneless beef chuck pot roast
1 tablespoon mild vegetable oil, such as canola
4 medium yellow onions, thinly sliced (6 cups)
1 cup apple juice or water

2 large garlic cloves, minced
1 tablespoon balsamic vinegar
1 tablespoon chopped fresh oregano leaves or 1 teaspoon dried, crumbled
1 tablespoon chopped fresh thyme leaves or 1 teaspoon dried, crumbled
   Salt, optional, and freshly ground black pepper to taste

PREP TIME: 20 MIN

COOK TIME: 8–10 HR ON LOW OR 4–5 HR ON HIGH

STAND TIME: 15 MIN

1. Put apples in a 3½-quart or larger crockery slow-cooker. Sprinkle with cinnamon.

2. Trim fat from roast. If necessary, cut roast into 2 pieces to fit into slow-cooker. In a large skillet, brown roast in oil over medium-high heat, turning roast to brown all sides, about 10 minutes.

3. Put roast on top of apples. Separate onions into rings and put on top of meat. In a small bowl, combine remaining ingredients and pour over meat and onions. Do not stir. Cover and cook on LOW for 8 to 10 hours or on HIGH for 4 to 5 hours.

4. Transfer meat to a carving platter. Let stand for 15 minutes before slicing. Serve with apples, onions, and any pan juices.

Per serving: 405 calories, 48 g protein, 13 g total fat (3.8 g saturated), 34 g carbohydrates, 82 mg sodium, 117 mg cholesterol, 4 g dietary fiber

SAUERBRATEN WITH GINGER GRAVY

MAKES 8 SERVINGS

Many Heartland states were settled by German immigrants. Sauerbraten is a tangy-sweet German pot roast that needs at least a day to marinate, so plan ahead. The tender, slow-cooked meat is delectable, and the gravy is nicely spiced, thickened by the gingersnaps. Serve it with lightly buttered thin egg noodles.

For a vegetable, steam a combination of cauliflower, zucchini, yellow summer squash, and whole garlic cloves. Toss with buttered rye bread crumbs and caraway seeds. ▶

SAUERBRATEN WITH GINGER GRAVY *(see previous page for photo and notes)*

1   3- to 4-pound boneless beef rump or sirloin tip roast
¾   cup cider vinegar
¾   cup dry red wine
2   tablespoons light brown sugar
1   teaspoon dry mustard
1   teaspoon salt

2   medium yellow onions, sliced (3 cups)
3   large garlic cloves, sliced
1   teaspoon whole black peppercorns
4   whole cloves
2   large bay leaves
1   cup sour cream
12   gingersnaps, crumbled (½ cup)

**PREP TIME:
20 MIN +
AT LEAST 24 HR
FOR MARINATING**

**COOK TIME:
10–12 HR ON LOW +
15 MIN ON HIGH TO
MAKE GRAVY OR
5¼–6¼ ON HIGH**

1. Trim excess fat from roast. Place in a deep ceramic or glass bowl. In a medium saucepan, whisk together vinegar, wine, brown sugar, dry mustard, and salt. Over medium high heat, bring to a simmer; do not boil. Pour over roast. Top with onions, garlic, peppercorns, cloves, and bay leaves. Cover and refrigerate for 24 to 36 hours, turning meat several times.

2. Remove roast from marinade and place in a 3½-quart or larger crockery slow-cooker. If necessary, cut roast into 2 pieces to fit. In a small saucepan, bring marinade to a full boil. Continue to boil for 1 minute. Pour marinade over roast; do not stir. Cover and cook on LOW for 10 to 12 hours or on HIGH for 5 to 6 hours. Transfer meat to a heated serving platter. Discard bay leaves.

3. Strain pan juices through a coarse sieve gently pressing vegetable to extract liquid. Skim off fat. Return 1 cup of pan juices to the slow-cooker.

4. If cooking on LOW, change setting to HIGH. Stir in sour cream and gingersnaps. Cook, uncovered, for 15 minutes, until heated through and thickened. Do not boil.

5. To serve, carve roast across the grain, spooning some of the gingersnap gravy over each serving.

Per serving: 386 calories, 41 g protein, 16 g total fat (6.7 g saturated), 16 g carbohydrates, 416 mg sodium, 130 mg cholesterol, 1 g dietary fiber

SHORT RIBS JARDINIERE

MAKES 4 SERVINGS

These savory short ribs are easy. Serve them with mashed turnips or buttered noodles. For a salad, toss a cornucopia of fresh garden greens and pass a pitcher of old-fashioned buttermilk dressing.

4 lean beef short ribs (about 3 pounds total)
1 tablespoon olive oil
1 medium yellow onion, chopped (1 cup)
2 large garlic cloves, minced
1 16-ounce can peeled tomatoes, chopped
   and juice reserved
½ cup beef stock (page 82) or canned
   low-sodium broth

½ tablespoon chopped fresh basil leaves
   or ½ teaspoon dried, crumbled
1 teaspoon chopped fresh thyme leaves
   or ¼ teaspoon dried, crumbled
2 tablespoons minced fresh flat-leaf parsley
   leaves for garnish

**PREP TIME:
20 MIN
COOK TIME:
8-10 HR ON LOW
OR 4-5 HR
ON HIGH**

1. In a large skillet, brown short ribs in oil over medium-high heat, turning to brown all sides, about 10 minutes. Transfer short ribs to a 4-quart or larger crockery slow-cooker.

2. In the same skillet, sauté onion and garlic until onion is wilted, about 4 minutes; spoon over short ribs. Add tomatoes and their juice, stock, basil, and thyme to slow-cooker. Do not stir. Cover and cook on LOW for 8 to 10 hours or on HIGH for 4 to 5 hours.

3. Transfer short ribs to a heated serving platter. Spoon on sauce and garnish with chopped parsley.

Per serving: 331 calories, 29 g protein, 20 g total fat (7.4 g saturated), 8 g carbohydrates, 247 mg sodium, 82 mg cholesterol, 2 g dietary fiber

STUFFED
CABBAGE ROLLS

MAKES 6 SERVINGS

Recipes for stuffed cabbage rolls are usually Hungarian or Swedish in origin. This one, however, is adapted from the recipe used by the South African cook at my sorority house while I was attending Kansas State University. Made from humble ingredients, these cabbage rolls are distinctive enough to serve at special family dinners.

The crockery slow-cooker allows these little cabbage packages to develop their full flavor for a delicious, earthy meal. You may substitute a mixture of ground pork and veal for the beef.

Accompany with a julienne of zucchini and summer squash, and offer a favorite Midwestern salad: chopped salad greens topped with thinly sliced white onions, coarsely chopped hard-cooked egg, pieces of crisp-cooked bacon, and crumbled Maytag Blue, the tangy blue cheese made in Newton, Iowa (see Sources, page 142).

If using a 3½-quart slow-cooker, prepare half of the recipe

CABBAGE ROLLS

- 12 large green cabbage leaves
- ¾ cup water
- 1 teaspoon butter
- ¼ teaspoon salt
- ¼ cup long-grain white rice
- 1¼ pounds lean ground beef
- 1 large egg, slightly beaten
- 1 large tart apple, such as Granny Smith or Northern Spy, peeled, cored, and minced (¾ cup)
- 1 small yellow onion, minced (½ cup)
- 1 large garlic clove, minced
- ⅓ cup chopped fresh dill or 1½ tablespoons dried dill weed
- 2 tablespoons chopped fresh flat-leaf parsley
  Salt, optional, and freshly ground
  black pepper to taste

TOMATO SAUCE

- 1 tablespoon olive oil
- 2 medium yellow onions, halved and thinly sliced (3 cups)
- 2 large garlic cloves, chopped
- 1 28-ounce can crushed tomatoes, undrained
- 3 tablespoons fresh lemon juice (1 lemon)
- 1 tablespoon hot paprika
- 1 teaspoon Worcestershire sauce

PREP TIME: 45 MIN
COOK TIME: 7–9 HR ON LOW OR 3½–4½ HR ON HIGH

1. Blanch cabbage leaves in boiling water for 3 minutes, until limp. Drain and rinse under cold water to stop the cooking process. Drain and set aside.

2. In a small saucepan, bring water, butter, and salt to a rapid boil. Add rice, reduce heat, cover, and cook for 15 to 20 minutes, until rice is tender and water is absorbed.

3. In a large bowl, combine cooked rice, beef, egg, apple, onion, garlic, dill, parsley, salt, and pepper. Mix well.

4. Place cabbage leaves on a large wooden board. Put ¼ cup of the beef mixture at the bottom of each leaf and roll up, folding in the sides and completely enclosing the filling. Set filled leaves aside.

5. **To make Tomato Sauce:** In a large skillet, heat oil over medium-high heat. Add onions and garlic; cook until onions are limp, about 4 minutes. Stir in remaining sauce ingredients and cook for 5 minutes. Transfer half of the tomato sauce to a 4-quart or larger crockery slow-cooker. Place the cabbage rolls, seam side down, in the sauce, making as many layers as necessary. Top with remaining sauce. Do not stir. Cover and cook on LOW for 7 to 9 hours or on HIGH for 3½ to 4½ hours.

6. Transfer cabbage rolls to a heated serving platter and spoon sauce over top.

Per 2-roll serving: 310 calories, 24 g protein, 13 g total fat (4.5 g saturated), 26 g carbohydrate, 410 mg sodium, 72 mg cholesterol, 4 g dietary fiber

SWISS STEAK—
KANSAS STYLE

MAKES 4 SERVINGS

Swiss steak is old-fashioned and very Midwestern. Made this way in a crockery slow-cooker, it's fork-tender and exceptionally delicious. Traditionally the flour is pounded into the steak prior to cooking, a step that's unnecessary when using a slow-cooker.

Oven-fried potatoes and steamed green beans complement the steak perfectly.

2½ tablespoons unbleached all-purpose flour
½ tablespoon chopped fresh thyme leaves or ½ teaspoon dried, crumbled
¼ teaspoon sweet paprika
   Salt, optional, and freshly ground black pepper to taste
2 pounds boneless beef round steak, cut 1-inch thick
1½ tablespoons Worcestershire sauce
1 tablespoon mild vegetable oil, such as canola

1 large garlic clove, minced
2 medium celery ribs, thinly sliced (1 cup)
2 medium yellow onions, thinly sliced (3 cups)
4 large plum tomatoes, thinly sliced crosswise (1½ cups)
½ cup beef stock (page 82) or canned low-sodium broth

**PREP TIME:
20 MIN**

**COOK TIME:
8–10 HR ON LOW
OR 4–5 HR
ON HIGH**

1. In a small bowl, combine flour, thyme, paprika, salt, and pepper. Cut the steak into 8 serving pieces. Using a pastry brush, baste steak pieces with Worcestershire sauce. Dredge meat in flour mixture.

2. In a large skillet, heat oil over medium-high heat. Add steak pieces and brown, about 5 minutes per side.

3. Transfer steak to a 3½-quart or larger crockery slow-cooker. Sprinkle garlic over steak; top with celery. Scatter onions over steak and top with tomatoes. Pour in stock. Do not stir. Cover and cook on LOW for 8 to 10 hours or on HIGH for 4 to 5 hours. If cooking on HIGH, stir once during last hour of cooking.

4. To serve, transfer steak and vegetables to a heated serving platter. Spoon on any pan juices and serve.

Per serving: 500 calories, 47 g protein, 28 g total fat (9.6 g saturated), 14 g carbohydrates, 195 mg sodium,
121 mg cholesterol, 2 g dietary fiber

LEMON VEAL WITH SHIITAKE MUSHROOMS AND DILL

MAKES 8 SERVINGS

Shiitake mushrooms, originally from Japan and Korea, are now being cultivated in Minnesota and Wisconsin. Here, fresh shiitakes provide a flavorful cooking base for a veal roast. The sauce is freshened with lots of lemon and fresh dill.

I can buy fresh shiitake mushrooms that are already cleaned and sliced at my supermarket. Another fresh mushroom could be used, but the meaty flavor of the shiitake mushroom greatly enhances this dish. In the Midwest, fennel is frequently mislabeled "sweet anise". Actually, fennel is sweeter than anise, and cooked fennel, as it appears in this recipe, is even lighter and more delicate in flavor.

For a special fall meal, serve this with rice, such as herbed Wehani rice. A long-grained basmati-type hybrid, Wehani turns a deep russet color when cooked and makes a nice change from wild rice. You'll find Wehani in larger supermarkets and natural foods stores. This recipe does not work well on HIGH.

1 pound fresh shiitake mushrooms, sliced (12 cups)

1 3-pound boneless veal shoulder roast, rolled and tied

1 large yellow onion, chopped (1½ cups)

1 medium carrot, peeled and chopped (¾ cup)

1 small leek, white part only, well rinsed and thinly sliced (½ cup)

1 small fennel bulb, trimmed and thinly sliced (1 cup)

1 medium celery rib, thinly sliced (½ cup)

⅓ cup chopped fresh dill or 1½ tablespoons dried dill weed
Salt, optional, and freshly ground black pepper to taste

2 cups chicken stock (page 52) or canned low-sodium broth

⅓ cup fresh lemon juice (2 large lemons)

3 tablespoons unbleached all-purpose flour

1 cup heavy cream

2 teaspoons grated lemon rind
Lemon slices for garnish

PREP TIME: 20 MIN

COOK TIME: 7½–9½ HR ON LOW + 20–25 MIN TO MAKE SAUCE

1. Arrange mushrooms in a 4-quart or larger crockery slow-cooker. Put veal roast on top of mushrooms. If necessary, cut the roast to fit into the slow-cooker. Surround with onion, carrot, leek, fennel, and celery. Add 3 tablespoons of the fresh dill or 1 tablespoon of the dill weed, salt, pepper, stock, and lemon juice. Cover and cook on LOW for 7 to 9 hours.

2. Transfer roast and mushrooms to a heated serving platter. Keep warm.

3. In a medium bowl, whisk together flour and heavy cream. Whisk in ½ cup of the hot pan juices. Add mixture to slow-cooker, whisking constantly. Add lemon rind and the remaining fresh dill or dill weed. Cover and continue to cook for 20 to 25 minutes.

4. Slice veal very thin and serve with some of the sauce, garnished with lemon slices.

Per serving: 419 calories, 47 g protein, 20 g total fat (9.2 g saturated), 13 g carbohydrates, 180 mg sodium, 207 mg cholesterol, 3 g dietary fiber

VEAL SHANKS BRAISED IN APPLE CIDER

MAKES 4 SERVINGS

A crockery slow-cooker simmers meaty veal shanks to perfection in apple cider, the sweet pressed juice of apples sold by most every Heartland apple grower.

Serve this with steamed white rice flavored with a pinch of saffron, into which you've thrown a handful of peas and slivers of fresh basil.

Don't try this recipe on HIGH; the shanks won't thoroughly absorb the delicious flavors. If using a 3½- or 4-quart slow-cooker, prepare half of the recipe.

4   veal shanks, cut 2½ inches long
     (about 3 pounds total)
     Salt, optional, and freshly ground
     black pepper to taste
2   tablespoons unbleached all-purpose
     flour
2   tablespoons olive oil
2   medium carrots, peeled and chopped
     (1½ cups)
1   large yellow onion, chopped
     (1½ cups)
1   medium celery rib, chopped (½ cup)
2   large shallots, minced (2 tablespoons)

2   large garlic cloves, minced
1   medium tomato, finely chopped
     (1 cup)
2   tablespoons tomato paste
½   tablespoon chopped fresh thyme
     leaves or ½ teaspoon dried, crumbled
1   teaspoon chopped fresh rosemary
     leaves or ¼ teaspoon dried, crumbled
1   cup sweet apple cider
1   cup beef stock (page 82) or canned
     low-sodium broth
2   tablespoons chopped fresh parsley for garnish

1. Season veal shanks with salt and pepper. Dredge in flour. In a large skillet, brown shanks in oil over medium-high heat, about 5 minutes per side.

2. Transfer browned shanks to a 5-quart or larger crockery slow-cooker. To same skillet, add carrots, onion, celery, shallots, and garlic. Cook, over medium high heat, stirring occasionally, until vegetables are soft, about 5 minutes. Add tomato, reserving 2 tablespoons for garnish. Stir in tomato paste, thyme, and rosemary. Add cider and stock. Bring to a boil. Spoon vegetable mixture over shanks in slow-cooker. Do not stir. Cover and cook on LOW for 8 to 10 hours. Remove shanks from cooking liquid. Keep warm.

3. Turn slow-cooker setting to HIGH and cook, uncovered, until liquids are thick, about 15 minutes. Spoon vegetables and sauce over shanks. Garnish with reserved tomatoes and the chopped parsley.

PREP TIME:
20 MIN
COOK TIME:
8–10 HR ON LOW
+ 15 MIN ON
HIGH

Per serving: 439 calories, 51 g protein, 16 g total fat (4.2 g saturated), 23 g carbohydrates, 230 mg sodium, 175 mg cholesterol, 3 g dietary fiber

HERBED LEG OF LAMB WITH VEGETABLES

MAKES 8 SERVINGS

Prized by today's trendy cooks and restaurant chefs, ramps (wild leeks) were well known to the early settlers of the Heartland, particularly in the northern regions. Here they are cooked with a boneless leg of lamb and other vegetables. My produce market carries ramps from March to June. Choose ones that are firm with bright-colored greenery. You can also use milder-flavored cultivated leeks. Add additional garlic since ramps have a stronger and more garlicky-onion flavor than the common leek.

A salad of mixed greens and crusty bread are the only accompaniments needed.

1   2½- to 3-pound boneless leg of lamb, rolled and tied
4   large garlic cloves, peeled and halved
2   tablespoons Dijon-style mustard
1   tablespoon chopped fresh rosemary leaves or 1 teaspoon dried, crumbled
1   tablespoon chopped fresh thyme leaves or 1 teaspoon dried, crumbled
    Salt, optional, and freshly ground black pepper to taste
6   medium ramps (wild leeks), white part only, well rinsed and cut in half lengthwise

3   large carrots, peeled and cut into 2-inch pieces
1   medium rutabaga, peeled and cut into 2-inch pieces
1   large russet potato, scrubbed and cut into 6 pieces
3   tablespoons fresh lemon juice (1 large lemon)
¼   cup water
    Sprigs fresh rosemary and fresh thyme for garnish

1. Using a small sharp knife, make 8 small slits at equal intervals in the lamb. Insert garlic halves in these slits. In a small bowl, mix mustard, rosemary, thyme, salt, and pepper. Rub this mixture over top of lamb. Place lamb in a 3½-quart or larger crockery slow-cooker.

2. Put ramps on top of lamb and add remaining vegetables. Sprinkle with lemon juice and pour water over all. Do not stir. Cover and cook on LOW for 8 to 9 hours or on HIGH for 4 to 4½ hours, until lamb is tender.

3. To serve, arrange lamb and vegetables on a heated serving platter. Garnish with sprigs of rosemary and thyme. If desired, skim off excess fat from pan juices and serve the herbed juices separately to spoon over the meat.

PREP TIME: 20 MIN

COOK TIME: 8–9 HR ON LOW OR 4–4½ HR ON HIGH

Per serving: 274 calories, 34 g protein, 9g total fat (3.2 g saturated), 13 g carbohydrates, 194 mg sodium, 100 mg cholesterol, 3 g dietary fiber

LAMB SHANKS AND WHITE BEANS

MAKES 4 SERVINGS

Meaty lamb shanks become fork-tender when simmered in a light tomato broth. The addition of beans and morels makes this a complete meal.

Michigan's fresh morels are legendary, but you can buy excellent dried morels in some supermarkets and by mail order (see Sources, page 142). Add a tossed salad and a fresh-baked fruit pie for dessert, and you're ready for company.

Both the shanks and the beans need long slow-cooking, so don't try this on HIGH. If using a 3½- or 4-quart slow-cooker, prepare half of the recipe.

½ pound dried Great Northern beans, rinsed and picked over

6 cups water

1¾ ounces dried morels or other dried mushroom

1 cup hot water

4 lamb shanks (about ¾ pound each)
Salt, optional, and freshly ground black pepper to taste

1 tablespoon olive oil

3 large garlic cloves, minced

1 cup dry red wine

2 sprigs fresh rosemary or 1 teaspoon dried, crumbled

2 large bay leaves

1 32-ounce can whole plum tomatoes, undrained

1 cup chicken stock (page 53) or canned low-sodium broth

¼ cup freshly grated Parmesan cheese for garnish
Chopped fresh parsley for garnish

PREP TIME: 25 MIN + AT LEAST 1¼ HR FOR SOAKING BEANS

COOK TIME: 8–9 HR ON LOW

1. In a 5-quart or larger crockery slow-cooker, soak beans in 6 cups water overnight or for at least 6 hours. Or put beans and water in a large pot and bring to a boil on top of the stove. Boil for 2 minutes, turn off heat, cover, and let stand 1 hour. Drain soaked beans and place in slow-cooker.

2. Meanwhile, soak morels in hot water for 30 minutes. Drain, reserving soaking liquid, and coarsely chop. Scatter mushrooms on top of beans.

3. Season lamb shanks with salt and pepper. In a large skillet, brown lamb shanks in oil over medium-high heat, about 5 minutes per side. Put shanks on top of beans and morels. Add garlic and wine to skillet and cook for about 2 minutes, scraping the bottom of the skillet with a wooden spoon to loosen any browned bits. Pour wine mixture over shanks.

4. Top shanks with rosemary, bay leaves, tomatoes, stock, and reserved mushroom soaking liquid. Do not stir. Cover and cook on LOW for 8 to 9 hours.

5. To serve, arrange some of the beans and vegetables around each shank on individual plates. Discard bay leaves. Spoon on the pan juices and sprinkle with Parmesan cheese and chopped parsley.

Per serving: 611 calories, 47 g protein, 20 g total fat (7.2 g saturated), 53 g carbohydrates, 584 mg sodium, 100 mg cholesterol, 15 g dietary fiber

CROCKERY HAM WITH BEER GLAZE

MAKES 8 SERVINGS

Since ham is high in fat, cooks everywhere are serving it less often. For a summer company dinner, however, there's nothing easier to prepare or more delicious than this crockery-cooked ham—and the slow-cooker will keep the kitchen cool!

Serve the ham with a red potato salad, a minty fresh pea salad dotted with small cubes of Colby cheese. Over a salad of just-picked tomatoes, slice and sprinkle chopped, toasted sunflower seeds and raspberry vinegar. End the meal with your favorite fresh fruit pie.

If using a 3½- or 4-quart slow-cooker, purchase a boneless ham.

1 5- to 6-pound fully cooked ham, bone-in shank half Whole cloves ½ cup mango chutney	½ cup firmly packed light brown sugar 1½ tablespoons Dijon-style mustard 12 ounces beer

PREP TIME:
30 MIN

COOK TIME:
5–6 HR ON LOW +
30 MIN ON HIGH OR
3–3½ HR ON HIGH

STAND TIME:
15 MIN

1. Peel skin from ham and trim the fat to a ¼-inch layer. Using a sharp knife, score the fat in a diamond pattern. Insert a whole clove into each intersection of the diamonds. Place ham on a metal rack or trivet in a 5-quart or larger crockery slow-cooker. Cover and cook on LOW for 5 to 6 hours or on HIGH for 2½ to 3 hours. Remove ham. Using tongs, remove metal rack from slow-cooker. Pour off and discard pan juices. Return ham to slow-cooker. If cooking on LOW, change setting to HIGH.

2. Place chutney in a small bowl and chop any large pieces of fruit. Stir in brown sugar, mustard, and beer. Spoon some of the chutney mixture over ham. Cover and continue to cook for 30 minutes, basting every 5 minutes with remaining chutney mixture.

3. Transfer ham to a heated carving platter. Keep warm and let stand for 15 minutes before thinly slicing. Transfer chutney mixture to a serving dish to spoon over ham.

Per serving: 415 calories, 51 g protein, 13 g total fat (4.4 g saturated), 18 g carbohydrates, 3,553 mg sodium, 118 mg cholesterol, 1 g dietary fiber

PORK CHOP AND STUFFING BAKE

M A K E S   6   S E R V I N G S

This recipe comes from my sister, Eileen. She takes the makings for this dish when she and her husband week-end with their motor home, where a crockery slow-cooker is a standard piece of cooking equipment. Serve this with steamed Brussels sprouts.

If using a 3½- quart or 4-quart slow-cooker, prepare half the recipe.

1 8-ounce package dry corn bread stuffing crumbs
2 large tart apples, such as Granny Smith, Northern Spy, or Ida Red, peeled, cored, and chopped
2 tablespoons chopped fresh sage leaves or ½ tablespoon dried, crumbled
1 tablespoon chopped fresh thyme leaves or 1 teaspoon dried, crumbled
   Salt, optional, and freshly ground black pepper to taste

6 tablespoons butter (¾ stick)
3 medium celery ribs, thinly sliced (1½ cups)
1 large yellow onion, chopped (1½ cups)
2 large garlic cloves, minced
1¼ cups chicken stock (page 53) or canned low-sodium broth
6 center-cut bone-in pork chops, well trimmed (about 2½ pounds total)
1 tablespoon mild vegetable oil, such as canola
⅓ cup pecan halves

1. In a large bowl, combine stuffing mix, apples, sage, thyme, salt, and pepper. In a large skillet over medium heat, melt butter. Add celery, onion, and garlic. Cook, stirring occasionally, until vegetables are limp but not browned, about 4 minutes. Add stuffing mixture to skillet. Stir and cook for another 2 minutes. Stir in stock. Remove from heat.

2. Place half of the stuffing mixture in a 5-quart or larger crockery slow-cooker.

3. In a large skillet, brown pork chops in oil over medium-high heat for 5 minutes, turning once. Arrange pork chops on top of stuffing. Cover with remaining stuffing mixture. Cover and cook on LOW for 6 to 8 hours or on HIGH for 3 to 4 hours.

4. When ready to serve, arrange pork chops at one end of a heated serving platter. Stir pecans into stuffing in slow-cooker. Spoon stuffing onto platter and serve.

PREP TIME: 20 MIN
COOK TIME: 6-8 HR ON LOW OR 3-4 HR ON HIGH

Per serving: 653 calories, 34 g protein, 38 g total fat (14.3 g saturated), 44 g carbohydrates, 721 mg sodium, 125 mg cholesterol, 2 g dietary fiber

PORKETTA

MAKES 6 SERVINGS

This recipe comes from my son Kevin, who's been interested in cooking since he was tall enough to reach the kitchen counter (with the help of a chair to stand on). He roasts this garlicky and crusty pork roast in the oven, but a crockery slow-cooker does it to perfection without heating up the kitchen.

If using a 3½- or 4-quart slow-cooker, prepare the potatoes on top of the stove or in the oven.

1   2½- to 3-pound boneless pork loin
⅓   cup freshly grated Parmesan cheese
¼   cup chopped fresh flat-leaf parsley
1½ tablespoons coarsely cracked black peppercorns
2   large garlic cloves, minced

1   teaspoon sugar
1   tablespoon olive oil
6   medium russet potatoes, scrubbed and quartered
    Hot paprika

1. Using the tip of a sharp knife, cut slits 1 inch long and ¼ inch deep all over the surface of the roast.

2. In a small bowl, combine Parmesan cheese, parsley, cracked peppercorns, garlic, and sugar. Rub mixture over the surface of the roast, making sure it gets into the slits.

3. In a large skillet, brown seasoned pork roast in oil over medium-high heat for 10 minutes, until well browned on all sides.

4. Place roast on a metal rack or trivet in a 5-quart or larger crockery slow-cooker. Sprinkle cut edges of potatoes with paprika and place potatoes around roast. Cover and cook on LOW for 8 to 10 hours or on HIGH for 4 to 5 hours.

5. Transfer roast to a carving board and let stand for 10 minutes before thinly slicing. Serve with potatoes and any pan juices.

PREP TIME: 15 MIN
COOK TIME: 8–10 HR ON LOW OR 4–5 HR ON HIGH
STAND TIME: 10 MIN

Per serving: 541 calories, 48 g protein, 27 g total fat (9.8 g saturated), 25 g carbohydrates, 205 mg sodium, 132 mg cholesterol, 2 g dietary fiber

SAUERKRAUT DINNER

MAKES 6 SERVINGS

So much of the Heartland was settled by people of German heritage, it's not unusual for Midwestern cooks to serve sauerkraut at least once a week with spareribs and other cuts of pork or in potatoes and dumplings.

I'm not overly fond of sauerkraut, but when it's prepared this way in a crockery slow-cooker, I could easily become addicted. Buy the sauerkraut in a glass jar or plastic bag from the refrigerated deli section of your market. It costs a little more, but it tastes so much fresher than canned sauerkraut.

2 medium russet potatoes, scrubbed and sliced ¼ inch thick (2 cups)
2 medium yellow onions, sliced and separated into rings (3 cups)
2 medium carrots, peeled and sliced ½ inch thick (1½ cups)
2 large garlic cloves, minced
1 14½-ounce can peeled tomatoes, undrained

1 32-ounce jar sauerkraut, drained
½ cup sweet apple cider or apple juice
½ teaspoon caraway seeds
½ teaspoon freshly ground black pepper
1½ pounds fully-cooked smoked sausage, such as kielbasa, cut into 6 pieces

PREP TIME: 15 MIN
COOK TIME: 7–9 HR ON LOW OR 3½–4½ HR ON HIGH

1. Put potatoes, onions, carrots, and garlic in a 5-quart or larger crockery slow-cooker. Drain off juices from tomatoes and set aside. Coarsely chop tomatoes and add to slow-cooker along with sauerkraut.
2. In a medium bowl, combine reserved tomato juice, cider, caraway seeds, and black pepper. Pour over sauerkraut. Do not stir. Top with sausage pieces. Cover and cook on LOW for 7 to 9 hours or on HIGH for 3½ to 4½ hours.
3. To serve, pile sauerkraut onto a platter and top with sausage pieces.

Per serving: 456 calories, 18 g protein, 31 g total fat (11.3 g saturated), 26 g carbohydrates, 2,052 mg sodium, 76 mg cholesterol, 6 g dietary fiber

VENISON WITH MORELS AND JUNIPER BERRIES

MAKES 6 SERVINGS

*Once the prize of the hunter only, venison is now being ranch-raised, making it more readily available at special-
ty markets and by mail order (see Sources, page 142). Milder than lamb, but more distinctive than beef, the deep
red venison meat is lean and low in cholesterol.*

*Juniper berries, the blue-black berries of an evergreen, are favored by northern Heartlanders when preparing
venison and game birds. Look for jars of dried juniper berries in the spice department of your supermarket.*

Serve this flavorful dish with a potato and turnip gratin and butter-browned Brussels sprouts.

This recipe doesn't work well on HIGH.

3 pounds boneless venison leg, cut into
   6 portions
2 tablespoons freshly cracked black peppercorns
2 large garlic cloves, minced
1 tablespoon fresh thyme leaves
   or 1 teaspoon dried, crumbled
3 tablespoons Dijon-style mustard
1½ cups beef stock (page 82) or canned
   low-sodium broth

2 tablespoons butter
½ pound fresh morels, coarsely chopped
   (4 cups), or 1¾ ounces dried, reconstituted
   in boiling water, drained, and coarsely chopped
¼ cup red wine vinegar
¼ cup brandy, optional
1 tablespoon dried juniper berries, crushed
   Salt, optional, and freshly ground
   black pepper to taste

1. Rub venison pieces with peppercorns, garlic, and thyme, then coat with mustard. Put in
a 3½-quart or larger crockery slow-cooker. Add ½ cup stock. Cover and cook on LOW for
8 to 10 hours.

2. Remove venison from slow-cooker and keep warm. Transfer any venison drippings to a
large skillet. Add butter to skillet and melt over medium heat. Stir in morels and cook,
uncovered, until their liquid is incorporated, about 5 minutes. Add vinegar and cook, uncovered, until sauce is reduced by half. Stir in remaining 1 cup stock and reduce by half again. Stir
in brandy and juniper berries. Cook for 2 to 3 minutes more. Taste and add salt and pepper.

3. Carve venison into ¼-inch slices. Spoon some of the sauce onto each serving and pass the remaining sauce in
a gravy boat to serve on the side.

**PREP TIME:
15 MIN**

**COOK TIME:
8–10 HR ON LOW +
25 MIN ON STOVE
FOR MAKING
SAUCE**

Per serving: 375 calories, 55 g protein, 11 g total fat (4.7 g saturated), 7 g carbohydrates, 341 mg sodium, 201 mg cholesterol, 1 g dietary fiber

VEGETARIAN DISHES

THE BASIS OF MANY OF MY VEGETARIAN RECIPES is a well-seasoned vegetable stock. A crockery slow-cooker makes this stock preparation almost effortless. The stock will keep in the refrigerator for up to three days, or it can be frozen for longer storage, up to three months. For an even richer flavor, boil the strained stock on top of the stove until it reduces by half.

You could also use a vegetarian bouillon cube that dissolves in hot water. If your supermarket doesn't carry the bouillon cubes, try a natural foods store or specialty food shop.

These recipes are designed to be flexible. All are sufficient enough to be the whole meal, or they can be served in smaller portions as part of a larger meal. For best results, you'll need a reliable supply of excellent quality produce. If your market, however, doesn't carry high-quality produce, you might want to start a kitchen garden or seek out a local source of farm-grown produce.

Follow the recipes closely, particularly in the cutting of the vegetables. Something as simple as the size or shape of an ingredient can change the appearance and taste of the finished dish. Both summer and winter vegetables respond well to slow-cooking, which allows the flavors to mingle and deepen.

Several of the recipes also call for beans, an important cash crop in the Heartland. Perfect for the slow-cooker, the bean recipes begin as a combination of humble ingredients that develops into a dish with delicate flavor and texture.

GARDENER'S STEW OVER COUSCOUS

MAKES 4 SERVINGS

By mid-June most every city and town in the Heartland has at least one farmers' open-air market, offering picked-that-day tomatoes, corn, sweet bell peppers, and squash. This vegetable stew is the kind of light supper to fix when these markets, or your own kitchen garden, are brimming with the bounty of summer.

Couscous is tiny pellets of semolina, coarsely ground durum wheat. It makes a perfect base for the colorful stew. Look for it in larger supermarkets or Middle Eastern markets.

2 medium yellow onions, chopped (2 cups)
4 large cloves garlic, minced
1 tablespoon olive oil
1 large red bell pepper, seeded and cut into thick strips
2 small Japanese eggplants, unpeeled and cut into 2-inch cubes
3 medium zucchini, halved and cut into 1-inch slices
4 medium tomatoes, coarsely chopped (4 cups)
½ cup tomato juice
1 tablespoon tomato paste
1 tablespoon chopped fresh oregano leaves or 1 teaspoon dried, crumbled

1 tablespoon fresh thyme leaves or 1 teaspoon dried, crumbled
Salt, optional, and freshly ground black pepper to taste
½ cup shelled fresh peas or ½ cup frozen baby peas, thawed

COUSCOUS

3 cups chicken stock (page 53) or canned low-sodium broth
1 tablespoon butter
Salt, optional
1 cup quick-cooking couscous
Sprigs fresh basil for garnish

PREP TIME: 25 MIN

COOK TIME: 7–8 HR ON LOW OR 3½–4 HR ON HIGH

1. Put onions and garlic in a 3½-quart or larger crockery slow-cooker. Drizzle with oil. Top with red pepper, eggplants, zucchini, and tomatoes.

2. In a measuring cup, combine tomato juice, tomato paste, oregano, thyme, salt, and pepper. Pour over vegetables. Do not stir. Cook on LOW for 7 to 8 hours or on HIGH for 3½ to 4 hours, gently stirring in the peas during the last 20 minutes when cooking on LOW or 10 minutes on HIGH.

3. Just before serving, prepare couscous. In a medium saucepan, bring stock, butter, and salt to a boil over high heat. Add couscous and stir; cover. Remove from heat and let stand for 5 minutes. Fluff with a fork.

4. To serve, line a large platter with couscous and top with vegetable stew. Garnish with sprigs of basil.

Per serving: 353 calories, 14 g protein, 9 g total fat (2.7 g saturated), 57 g carbohydrates, 249 mg sodium, 8 mg cholesterol, 9 g dietary fiber

VEGETABLE STOCK

MAKES 3 QUARTS NON-REDUCED STOCK

PREP TIME: 25 MIN • COOK TIME: 8-10 HR ON LOW • OR 5-6 HR ON HIGH

If using a 3½- or 4-quart slow-cooker, prepare half of the recipe.

3 large carrots, peeled and quartered
2 large tomatoes, cored and cut into eighths
1 large yellow onion, peeled and quartered
1 parsnip, peeled and quartered
1 small head green cabbage, chopped
1 large russet potato, scrubbed and quartered
1 large sweet potato, scrubbed and quartered
1 large celery rib, quartered
1 large leek, white with 1 inch pale-green tops, well rinsed and cut in half lengthwise

3 large garlic cloves, sliced
2 tablespoons chopped fresh basil leaves or 2 teaspoons dried, crumbled
1 tablespoon fresh thyme leaves or 1 teaspoon dried, crumbled
4 sprigs fresh flat-leaf parsley
3 quarts water
2 teaspoons salt
1 teaspoon whole black peppercorns

1. Put all ingredients in a 5-quart or larger crockery slow-cooker. Do not stir. Cover and cook on LOW for 8 to 10 hours or on HIGH for 4 to 5 hours.

2. Strain stock into colander over large bowl, pressing vegetables to extract as much liquid as possible. Discard vegetables. If desired, cook stock, uncovered, in saucepan on top of stove over high heat until reduced by half.

3. Refrigerate, covered tightly, for up to 3 days or freeze for up to 3 months.

Per 1-cup serving: 25 calories, 1 g protein, trace total fat (0 saturated), 5 g carbohydrates, 304 mg sodium, 0 cholesterol, 1 g dietary fiber

LENTIL SOUP WITH TOMATOES AND GARLIC

MAKES 8 SERVINGS

Nothing is more warming than a crock of simmering soup on a sub-zero night. This hearty soup is blessed with fresh herbs, which are fortunately available year-round at the supermarket. Serve this soup with some crusty bread, a hunk of sharp Cheddar cheese, and a bottle of your favorite red wine.

If using a 3½- or 4-quart slow-cooker, prepare half of the recipe.

2¼ cups green lentils, washed and picked over

2 quarts vegetable stock (page 119) or broth prepared from vegetable bouillon cubes

1 large yellow onion, chopped (1½ cups)

3 large garlic cloves, thinly sliced

2 medium carrots, peeled and minced (1½ cups)

2 medium celery ribs, minced (1 cup)

1 32-ounce can Italian plum tomatoes, undrained

¼ cup chopped fresh flat-leaf parsley

½ tablespoon chopped fresh dill or ½ teaspoon dried dill weed

½ tablespoon chopped fresh marjoram leaves or ½ teaspoon dried, crumbled

½ tablespoon fresh thyme leaves or ½ teaspoon dried, crumbled

2 large bay leaves
Salt, optional, and freshly ground black pepper to taste

2 tablespoons balsamic vinegar

½ cup sour cream or plain yogurt for garnish

3 green onions, white and green parts, thinly sliced, for garnish

**PREP TIME:
20 MIN
COOK TIME:
10–12 HR ON LOW
OR 5–6 HR
ON HIGH**

1. Put lentils in a 5-quart or larger crockery slow-cooker. Add remaining ingredients in the order given, except vinegar and garnishes (vinegar added early in the cooking process will actually toughen the lentils). Do not stir. Cover and cook on LOW for 10 to 12 hours or on HIGH for 5 to 6 hours. If cooking on HIGH, stir once during last hour of cooking.

2. Just before serving, stir in balsamic vinegar. Discard bay leaves. Ladle into soup bowls. Garnish with a dollop of sour cream and a sprinkling of sliced green onions.

Per serving: 276 calories, 18 g protein, 4 g total fat (2.1 g saturated), 45 g carbohydrates, 553 mg sodium, 7 mg cholesterol, 9 g dietary fiber

COOKING BEANS

Many of the vegetarian recipes contain beans; specific cooking instructions are given in each recipe. If you live at a high altitude, you will need to boil the beans briefly before soaking them overnight. Most bean recipes may be cooked longer than the times indicated or may be cooked one day and reheated in the slow-cooker for serving the next day.

RED KIDNEY BEAN CHILI

MAKES 6 SERVINGS

Chili at our house is usually made with red kidney beans instead of the more traditional pintos. In a crockery slow-cooker the beans become pleasantly tender. This meatless chili is nicely spiced, and the crumbled goat cheese adds a flavorful garnish. For more than ten years, Heartland cheesemakers have been producing chèvre, fresh cheese made from goat's milk. The delightful mild-flavored goat cheese will melt quickly and evenly into the chili and makes a nice change from Cheddar.

If using a 3½- or 4-quart slow-cooker, prepare half of the recipe.

1 pound dried red kidney beans, rinsed and picked over

6 cups water

1 large red onion, minced (1½ cups)

1 large yellow onion, minced (1½ cups)

4 large garlic cloves, minced

1 large red bell pepper, seeded and cut into ½-inch pieces (1½ cups)

1 large yellow bell pepper, seeded and cut into ½-inch pieces (1½ cups)

3 jalapeño chile peppers, seeded and minced

2 tablespoons chili powder

1 tablespoon ground cumin

2 tablespoons chopped fresh oregano leaves or 2 teaspoons dried, crumbled

1 32-ounce can Italian plum tomatoes, undrained

1 quart vegetable stock (page 119) or broth prepared from vegetable bouillon cubes

2 cups fresh corn kernels or 1 10-ounce package frozen, thawed and drained Chopped fresh cilantro for garnish

¼ pound fresh goat cheese, crumbled, for garnish

1. In a 5-quart or larger crockery slow-cooker, soak beans in water overnight or for at least 6 hours. Or put beans and water in a large pot and bring to a boil on top of the stove. Boil for 2 minutes, turn off heat, cover, and let stand 1 hour. Drain beans and place in slow-cooker.

2. Add remaining ingredients except corn, cilantro, and goat cheese. Do not stir. Cover and cook on LOW for 8 to 10 hours or on HIGH for 4 to 5 hours. If cooking on LOW, change setting to HIGH. Stir in corn and cook, covered, about 15 minutes.

3. To serve, ladle into individual soup bowls. Garnish each serving with chopped cilantro and goat cheese.

**PREP TIME:
20 MIN + AT
LEAST 1¼ HR FOR
SOAKING BEANS

COOK TIME:
8-10 HR ON LOW +
15 MIN ON HIGH
OR 4¼-5¼ HR
ON HIGH**

Per serving: 458 calories, 26 g protein, 8 g total fat (4.4 saturated), 75 g carbohydrates, 615 mg sodium, 15 mg cholesterol, 20 g dietary fiber

SLOW-ROASTED VEGETABLES

MAKES 6 SERVINGS

Recently rediscovered by restaurants and home cooks across the nation, slow-roasting vegetables is a cooking technique as old as the Heartland. The Native Americans of the Midwest were seen roasting vegetables under thick layers of grass by the early explorers, and pioneer housewives roasted vegetables in the kitchen hearth, buried under a thick layer of ashes.

A crockery slow-cooker greatly intensifies the flavor of these vegetables. Serve them over hot cooked linguine that has been tossed with a little olive oil. If you don't have a hand-held grater for the Parmesan cheese, you can shave it with a vegetable peeler onto the finished dish.

1 small winter squash, such as butternut, acorn, sweet dumpling, or delicata (about 1 pound), seeded and cut into 2-inch wedges
12 whole baby carrots, peeled
3 baby Japanese eggplants, unpeeled and halved lengthwise
12 small white onions, peeled
6 plum tomatoes, stemmed
2 tablespoons olive oil
3 tablespoons chopped fresh flat-leaf parsley

1 tablespoon fresh thyme leaves or 1 teaspoon dried, crumbled
¼ teaspoon crushed red pepper
Salt, optional, and freshly ground black pepper to taste
½ pound fresh greens, such as mustard, spinach, or Swiss chard
2 ounces Parmesan cheese, freshly grated or shaved (½ cup)
¼ cup chopped fresh basil leaves for garnish

1. Arrange the squash, carrots, eggplants, onions, and tomatoes in a 3½-quart or larger crockery slow-cooker. Drizzle with olive oil; sprinkle with herbs, crushed red pepper, salt, and pepper. Cover and cook on LOW for 7 to 8 hours or on HIGH for 3½ to 4 hours.
2. Meanwhile, wash greens and remove any tough stem ends. If cooking on LOW, change setting to HIGH. Add greens to slow-cooker and continue to cook, covered, until greens wilt, about 5 minutes.
3. To serve, spoon vegetables and broth into individual wide, shallow soup bowls. Top each serving with shavings of Parmesan and sprinkle with basil.

PREP TIME: 20 MIN

COOK TIME: 7–8 HR ON LOW + 5 MIN ON HIGH OR 3½–4 HR + 5 MIN ON HIGH

Per serving: 181 calories, 8 g protein, 8 g total fat (2.6 g saturated), 22 g carbohydrates, 204 mg sodium, 7 mg cholesterol, 7 g dietary fiber

SPICY CORN CHOWDER

MAKES 6 SERVINGS

My dad grew some of the sweetest corn I've every tasted, the kernels snug on the cob, plump, and juicy. In the summer months, when you can buy corn like that, omit the honey from this recipe. Then cut the kernels from the cob just before adding it to the slow-cooker, about 20 minutes before the chowder has finished cooking.

Other times of the year, when you are using frozen corn, you'll need the honey since the corn's natural sugars turn to starch once it's cut from the cob and frozen.

1 large yellow onion, chopped (1½ cups)
3 large garlic cloves, minced
1 large yellow bell pepper, seeded and chopped (1½ cups)
1 large russet potato, scrubbed and diced (1½ cups)
2 medium celery ribs, thinly sliced (1 cup)
1 14½-ounce can crushed tomatoes, undrained
1 4-ounce can diced green chiles, undrained
2 cups vegetable stock (page 119) or broth prepared from vegetable bouillon cubes
¼ teaspoon crushed red pepper, or to taste
⅛ teaspoon liquid green or red hot pepper sauce, or to taste

Salt, optional, and freshly ground black pepper to taste
Corn kernels cut from 6 medium ears (3 cups) or 3 cups frozen kernels
1 tablespoon honey (if using frozen corn)
2 tablespoons unbleached all-purpose flour
2 tablespoons butter, at room temperature
½ cup half-and-half
Crumbled tortilla chips for garnish
Sprigs fresh cilantro for garnish
Liquid green or red hot pepper sauce for garnish

PREP TIME: 20 MIN
COOK TIME: 6–8 HR ON LOW + 15 MIN ON HIGH OR 3¼–4¼ HR ON HIGH

1. Put onion in a 3½-quart or larger crockery slow-cooker. Top with garlic, bell pepper, potato, celery, crushed tomatoes with their juice, green chiles, stock, crushed red pepper, ⅛ teaspoon liquid green hot pepper sauce, salt, and pepper. If using fresh corn, wait to add it later. If using frozen corn, add it now along with the honey. Do not stir. Cover and cook on LOW for 6 to 8 hours or on HIGH for 3 to 4 hours.

2. If cooking on LOW, change setting to HIGH. In a small bowl, combine flour and butter to form a paste. Stir into the soup. If using fresh corn, stir in the corn kernels. Cook, uncovered, stirring occasionally, for another 10 minutes, until soup is thickened and corn is tender. Gradually stir in the half-and-half. Heat for another 5 minutes.

3. Ladle into soup bowls. Garnish each serving with tortilla chips and cilantro. Offer additional liquid hot pepper sauce to sprinkle onto the chowder if desired.

Per serving: 209 calories, 6 g protein, 8 g total fat (4.1 g saturated), 34 g carbohydrates, 369 mg sodium, 18 mg cholesterol, 5 g dietary fiber

TEN-BEAN CASSEROLE

MAKES 8 SERVINGS

Beans are an important Heartland crop, particularly in Michigan—the world's largest producer of navy beans and a significant supplier of black beans, cranberry beans, and red kidney beans. Mix and match the beans for this recipe as you like; you'll need a total of 2½ cups.

Since I keep all of these beans in my pantry, I would use ¼ cup of each kind. The combination of flavors is truly wonderful. I can buy all of these beans in my supermarket, but you may need to look for some of the more unusual ones at your natural foods store.

If using a 3½- or 4-quart slow-cooker, prepare half the recipe.

2½ cups mixed dried beans (choose from azuki beans, black beans, black-eyed peas, chick peas, cranberry beans, kidney beans, lima beans, navy beans, pink beans, and pinto beans)

6 cups water

5 cups vegetable stock (page 119) or broth prepared from vegetable bouillon cubes

2 medium yellow onions, chopped (2 cups)

1 medium red bell pepper, seeded and chopped (1 cup)

1 14½-ounce can crushed tomatoes, undrained

3 large garlic cloves, minced

¼ cup firmly packed light brown sugar

¼ cup Worcestershire sauce

2 tablespoons chili powder

½ tablespoon cumin seeds

½ tablespoon celery seeds

½ teaspoon liquid red hot pepper sauce, or to taste

Salt, optional, and freshly ground black pepper to taste

CONDIMENTS

4 green onions with some green tops, thinly sliced (½ cup)

1 medium celery rib, thinly sliced (½ cup)

1 small tomato, finely chopped (½ cup)

1 large lemon, cut into 8 wedges

Freshly ground black pepper

1. Rinse and pick over beans. In a 5-quart or larger crockery slow-cooker, soak beans in water to cover overnight or for at least 6 hours. Or put beans and water in a large pot and bring to a boil on top of the stove. Boil for 2 minutes, turn off heat, cover, and let stand 1 hour. Drain beans and place in the slow-cooker.

2. Add stock along with the remaining ingredients except condiments. Stir well. Cover and cook on LOW for 10 to 12 hours or on HIGH for 5 to 6 hours. If cooking on HIGH, stir once during last hour of cooking.

3. If a thicker soup is desired, mash beans lightly with a potato masher. To serve, transfer beans to a heated serving dish. Pass condiments in separate bowls for seasoning beans.

PREP TIME: 25 MIN + 1¼ HR FOR SOAKING BEANS

COOK TIME: 10–12 HR ON LOW OR 5–6 HR ON HIGH

Per serving: 274 calories, 15 g protein, 2 g total fat (0.4 saturated), 53 g carbohydrates, 415 mg sodium, 0 cholesterol, 15 g dietary fiber

TOMATO MINESTRONE

MAKES 8 SERVINGS

At the turn of the century thousands of Italians flocked into Chicago and the other cities and towns of Illinois, seeking a better life. Since this recipe calls for rice and peas (not beans), it is typical of the minestrone made by Italians who emigrated from the north around Milan.

If using a 3½- or 4-quart slow-cooker, prepare half of the recipe.

1 large yellow onion, chopped (1½ cups)
1 large garlic clove, minced
1 large carrot, coarsely chopped (1 cup)
2 medium celery ribs, thinly sliced (1 cup)
½ pound Swiss chard, coarsely chopped (2 cups)
½ cup long-grain white rice
2 pounds fresh plum tomatoes, coarsely chopped (3 cups)
6 cups vegetable stock (page 117) or broth prepared from vegetable bouillon cubes
3 sprigs fresh thyme or ¼ teaspoon dried leaves, crumbled

2 sprigs fresh oregano or ⅛ teaspoon dried leaves, crumbled
1 large bay leaf
1 cup dried rigatoni or ziti pasta (about 5 ounces), cooked according to package directions for 5 minutes and drained
1 10-ounce package frozen peas, thawed
¼ cup freshly grated Parmesan cheese (1 ounce)

1. Put all of the ingredients in the order listed except the pasta, peas, and Parmesan into a 5-quart or larger crockery slow-cooker. Do not stir. Cover and cook on LOW for 7 to 9 hours or on HIGH for 3½ to 4½ hours.

2. If cooking on LOW, change setting to HIGH. Stir in pasta and peas. Cover and cook for 15 minutes, until pasta is tender. Discard bay leaf.

3. Ladle into individual bowls. Garnish each serving with Parmesan.

PREP TIME:
25 MIN
COOK TIME:
7–9 HR ON LOW +
15 MIN ON HIGH
OR 3¾–4¾ HR
ON HIGH

Per serving: 205 calories, 9 g protein, 2 g total fat (0.8 g saturated), 40 g carbohydrates, 435 mg sodium, 3 mg cholesterol, 5 g dietary fiber

VEGETABLE BARLEY STEW

MAKES 6 SERVINGS

Barley is one of the crops I grow on my farm in western Kansas. A grain belonging to the grass family, it cooks to just the right texture in a crockery slow-cooker.

A pesto made with sun-dried tomatoes in a food processor or blender adds an interesting finish.

2 large garlic cloves, minced
1 tablespoon olive oil
2 medium tomatoes, chopped (2 cups)
1 large yellow onion, quartered and sliced (2 cups)
1 medium celery root, peeled and thinly sliced (2 cups)
1 cup barley, well rinsed
2 tablespoons chopped fresh basil leaves or 2 teaspoons dried, crumbled
2½ cups tomato juice

3 tablespoons fresh lemon juice (1 large lemon)
½ head cauliflower, separated into small florets (2 cups)
⅓ cup low-fat plain yogurt for garnish

PESTO

12 sun-dried tomatoes packed in oil, drained
2 large garlic cloves, peeled
3 tablespoons olive oil
1 tablespoon chopped fresh basil leaves or 1 teaspoon dried, crumbled

PREP TIME:
20 MIN

COOK TIME:
6–8 HR ON LOW
OR 3–4 HR
ON HIGH

1. In a large skillet, cook garlic in oil over low heat until garlic is soft, about 4 minutes. Add tomatoes and onion. Cook for 5 minutes.

2. Transfer garlic-tomato mixture to a 3½-quart or larger crockery slow-cooker. Top with celery root, barley, and basil. Add tomato and lemon juices. Do not stir. Cover and cook on LOW for 6 to 8 hours or on HIGH for 3 to 4 hours, adding cauliflower florets during the last 30 minutes if cooking on LOW or 15 minutes if cooking on HIGH.

3. Just before serving, put all pesto ingredients in a food processor or blender. Process for about 15 seconds, until ingredients are just mixed but not finely chopped.

4. Spoon stew into shallow soup plates. Garnish each serving with a dollop of yogurt and some of the pesto.

Per serving: 284 calories, 7 g protein, 11 g total fat (1.7 g saturated), 43 g carbohydrates, 443 mg sodium, 1 mg cholesterol, 9 g dietary fiber

WILD RICE VEGETABLE BAKE

MAKES 8 SERVINGS

The exact time for cooking wild rice in a crockery slow-cooker depends on the dryness of the kernels of rice and whether you like wild rice slightly chewy or prefer it puffed and very tender. Check the rice after 6 hours of cooking the first time you make this dish and thereafter adjust the cooking time to your preference. (But don't try to speed things along by using the HIGH setting; the rice won't cook.)

You can substitute dried cranberries, chopped dried apricots, or golden raisins for the dried cherries.

If using a 3½- or 4-quart slow-cooker, prepare half of the recipe.

1½ cups wild rice, rinsed
1 large butternut squash (about 3 pounds)
1 large yellow onion, peeled and cut into 6 wedges
1 pound fresh button mushrooms, halved
1 medium carrot, peeled and sliced (¾ cup)
2 small turnips (about ½ pound total), peeled and each cut into 6 wedges

6 cups vegetable stock (page 117) or broth prepared with vegetable bouillon cubes
3 tablespoons fresh lemon juice (1 large lemon)
2 tablespoons butter or light olive oil
1 tablespoon chopped fresh marjoram leaves or 1 teaspoon dried, crumbled
Salt, optional, and freshly ground black pepper to taste
½ cup dried cherries

PREP TIME: 15 MIN

COOK TIME: 6-8 HR ON LOW

1. Put rice in a 5-quart or larger crockery slow-cooker. Cut squash in half lengthwise, remove seeds, and peel. Cut each half into quarters and put on top of rice.

2. Add onion, mushrooms, carrot, and turnips. Pour in stock and lemon juice. Dot with butter or drizzle with olive oil. Sprinkle on marjoram, salt, and pepper. Do not stir. Cover and cook on LOW for 6 to 8 hours.

3. A half hour before serving, stir in dried cherries. Cook, covered, until rice is done.

Per serving: 253 calories, 8 g protein, 4 g total fat (2.0 g saturated), 52 g carbohydrates, 314 mg sodium, 8 mg cholesterol, 7g dietary fiber

WINTER VEGETABLE STEW

MAKES 4 SERVINGS

Winter is a harsh season in the Heartland. When it seems like the cold weather will never end, prepare this warming vegetable stew.

To make this dish visually attractive, cut the vegetables into large pieces. The vegetables can be varied according to what you have on hand, but be sure to include plenty of carrots and plum tomatoes for their bright color and sweet flavor. My market sells vine-ripened organic plum tomatoes all winter, but you can use drained, canned plum tomatoes with excellent results.

3 medium carrots, peeled, cut in half lengthwise, and cut into 3-inch lengths

2 medium parsnips, peeled, cut in half lengthwise, and cut into 3-inch lengths

4 medium celery ribs, cut into 3-inch lengths

2 medium leeks, white part only, well rinsed and cut into 3-inch lengths

1 medium onion, peeled and cut into eighths

2 large garlic cloves, peeled and quartered

2 small thin-skinned potatoes, scrubbed and quartered

¼ pound firm button mushrooms

2 small turnips, peeled and quartered

4 fresh plum tomatoes, cut in half lengthwise

1 large lemon, quartered

6 sprigs fresh flat-leaf parsley

1¼ cups dry white wine

2 tablespoons soy sauce

1 tablespoon fresh thyme leaves or 1 teaspoon dried, crumbled

1 teaspoon fresh rosemary leaves or ¼ teaspoon dried, crumbled

½ medium head green cabbage, cored and quartered

1. Arrange all of the vegetables except cabbage in a 3½-quart or larger crockery slow-cooker, layering them in the order given. Top with lemon quarters and parsley.

2. In a measuring cup, combine wine, soy sauce, and herbs. Pour over vegetables. Do not stir. Cover and cook on LOW for 8 to 10 hours or on HIGH for 4 to 5 hours.

3. If cooking on LOW, change setting to HIGH. Add cabbage and cook, covered, for 30 minutes, until cabbage is just tender.

4. Discard lemon and parsley before spooning vegetables and broth into wide, shallow soup bowls to serve.

PREP TIME:
35 MIN

COOK TIME:
8–10 HR ON LOW
+ 30 MIN ON HIGH
OR 4¹/₂–5¹/₂ HR
ON HIGH

Per serving: 263 calories, 7 g protein, 1 g total fat (0 saturated), 49 g carbohydrates, 654 mg sodium, 0 cholesterol, 12 g dietary fiber

DESSERTS

FOR EVERYTHING FROM POACHED DRIED FRUITS to serve warm over vanilla ice cream to decadent pudding cakes that will stir up childhood memories, your slow-cooker is the answer to making luscious, down-home desserts with a minimum of fuss that are reminiscent of a more leisurely time.

With the addition of a small round rack or metal trivet inside your slow-cooker, you can even "bake" a rich custard full of vanilla, nutmeg, and eggs or steam an old-fashioned holiday pudding tart with cranberries that becomes more mellow and moist with time. Just measure your slow-cooker before purchasing a special mold or pan for "baking" these desserts. For best results, use the pan size called for in the recipes.

Be sure to use the temperature setting called for in the recipe. Some work only on LOW, others only on HIGH.

In my grandmother's day, desserts were made with what was easily available–whatever fruits and nuts were grown on the farm or limited spices on the rack. Today's cooks can shop the world at their local supermarket.

Pudding cakes, one dessert that a slow-cooker does quite well, dates back to Colonial times. Lemon and orange are the more classic flavors, but if you love chocolate, the version here is wonderfully gooey and especially easy to make.

After you've savored this sampling of desserts, consult your slow-cooker's manufacturer's instructions on how to adapt some of your own favorite recipes to the crockery slow-cooking way of dessert making.

BAKED RICE CUSTARD

MAKES 6 SERVINGS

An old-fashioned dessert that's quite rich but so good. If you really feel like splurging, serve the custard topped with whipped cream and a few of the season's berries alongside.

This recipe does not work well on HIGH.

Butter for greasing soufflé dish
½ cup short-grain white rice
2 cups whole evaporated milk
3 large eggs, slightly beaten
½ cup sugar

1 teaspoon vanilla extract
⅛ teaspoon salt
⅓ cup golden raisins
Ground cinnamon
Whipped cream, optional

**PREP TIME:
20 MIN
COOK TIME:
3½–4 HR ON LOW
STAND TIME:
20 MIN**

1. Butter a 1-quart soufflé dish that will fit inside your 3½-quart or larger crockery slow-cooker. Place a metal rack or trivet in the slow-cooker.
2. Cook rice according to package directions.
3. While rice is cooking, in a large bowl, combine evaporated milk, eggs, sugar, vanilla, salt, and raisins. Stir in cooked rice. Pour mixture into prepared soufflé dish. Sprinkle with cinnamon. Cover top with aluminum foil.
4. Place soufflé dish on the rack and carefully fill slow-cooker with hot water to reach about halfway up the side of the dish. Cover and cook on LOW for 3½ to 4 hours, until a tester inserted near the center of custard comes out clean.
5. Remove soufflé dish from slow-cooker. Let stand for 20 minutes before serving with whipped cream, if desired.

Per serving: 300 calories, 10 g protein, 9 g total fat (4.7 saturated), 45 g carbohydrates, 167 mg sodium, 131 mg cholesterol, 1 g dietary fiber

BLUEBERRY-PEACH CAKE

MAKES 6 SERVINGS

This is a homey dessert, filled with luscious ripe peaches and sweet blueberries. The dessert forms a cake-like topping as it bakes. Serve it hot with a pitcher of rich cream and a pot of strong coffee.

This recipe does not work well on LOW.

1½ cups unbleached all-purpose flour
1½ cups granulated sugar
1½ teaspoons baking powder
½ teaspoon salt
½ teaspoon ground cinnamon
3 large eggs, slightly beaten
3 tablespoons mild vegetable oil, such as canola
3 tablespoons whole milk

6 medium ripe fresh peaches (about 1½ pounds)
2 tablespoons fresh lemon juice
1 teaspoon grated lemon rind
1 pint fresh blueberries, rinsed and picked over (2 cups)
¾ cup water
2 tablespoons light brown sugar
Light cream or half-and-half, optional

1. In a medium bowl, combine flour, 1 cup of the sugar, baking powder, salt, and cinnamon. In a small bowl, whisk eggs until frothy. Add oil and milk, whisking until smooth. Make a well in the center of the flour mixture and pour in egg mixture. Stir just until evenly moistened. Do not overmix. Spread batter in the bottom of a 3½- or 4-quart crockery slow-cooker.

2. Peel and pit peaches. Cut peaches into thick slices and toss with lemon juice and rind. Arrange peach slices on top of batter and sprinkle with blueberries.

3. In a small saucepan over medium-high heat, combine remaining ½ cup sugar and the water. Bring to a boil. Pour over fruit. Sprinkle with brown sugar. Do not mix. Cover and cook on HIGH for 2 to 2½ hours or until a tester inserted near center of cake comes out clean. Let stand for at least 30 minutes before serving.

4. Spoon cake into individual dessert bowls and serve with cream, if desired.

PREP TIME:
20 MIN
COOK TIME:
2–2½ HR ON HIGH
STAND TIME:
30 MIN

Per serving: 448 calories, 8 g protein, 10 g total fat (1.5 g saturated), 95 g carbohydrates, 340 mg sodium, 107 mg cholesterol, 4 g dietary fiber

CROCKERY STEWED FRUITS

MAKES 12 SERVINGS

Nowadays most supermarkets carry a wonderful assortment of dried fruits in their produce section. The long slow-cooking gives the fruit an incredible depth of flavor. You can vary the recipe according to your fruit preference and what's available. Once you've tried one combination, you can start all over to combine another assortment of fruits, thus creating a new dessert.

Serve the fruit over vanilla ice cream or thin slices of pound cake.

8 cups mixed dried fruits (combination of pears, peaches, nectarines, cherries, figs, cranberries, and prunes)
½ cup sugar
3 cups water
⅓ cup fresh orange juice (1 medium orange)

3 tablespoons fresh lemon juice (1 large lemon)
3 2-inch strips of orange rind
3 2-inch strips of lemon rind
¼ teaspoon ground nutmeg
2 cinnamon sticks
6 whole cloves

1. Put dried fruit in a 3½-quart or larger crockery slow-cooker. Sprinkle with sugar. Combine water, orange juice, and lemon juice. Pour over fruit. Add orange and lemon rind and nutmeg. Stir to mix well. Place cinnamon sticks and cloves in a spice bag. Add to slow-cooker. Cover and cook on LOW for 7 to 9 hours or on HIGH for 3½ to 4½ hours. Remove spice bag.
2. Stir fruit mixture and spoon warm or chilled over ice cream or pound cake, if desired.

PREP TIME: 15 MIN
COOK TIME: 7-9 HR ON LOW OR 3½-4½ HR ON HIGH

Per serving: 307 calories, 3 g protein, 1 g total fat (0 saturated), 82 g carbohydrates, 7 mg sodium, 0 cholesterol, 9 g dietary fiber

HAZELNUT-CHOCOLATE PUDDING CAKE

MAKES 8 SERVINGS

Recipes for pudding cakes appeared in cookbooks published over a hundred years ago. These early American cakes were frequently flavored with rose water or a sweet wine.

This decadent chocolate version is flavored with hazelnut liqueur. If you prefer, you can add a teaspoon of vanilla extract to the second layer in place of the liqueur.

This recipe does not work well on LOW.

FIRST LAYER

- 1½ cups unbleached all-purpose flour
- ¾ cup sugar
- 3 tablespoons unsweetened cocoa powder
- 2 teaspoons baking powder
- ½ teaspoon salt
- ¾ cup whole milk
- 3 tablespoons butter, melted
- 1½ teaspoons vanilla extract
- 6 ounces semisweet chocolate, coarsely chopped
- ¾ cup chopped hazelnuts

SECOND LAYER

- 1 cup sugar
- ⅓ cup unsweetened cocoa powder
- ¼ cup hazelnut liqueur, optional
- 1½ cups boiling water
  - Whipped cream, optional
  - Chocolate curls, optional
  - Ground cinnamon, optional

PREP TIME: 20 MIN

COOK TIME: 2–2½ HR ON HIGH

1. In a medium bowl, combine flour, sugar, cocoa powder, baking powder, and salt. In a small bowl, whisk together milk, butter, and vanilla. Make a well in the center of flour mixture and pour in milk mixture. Stir just until evenly moistened. Do not overmix. Fold in chocolate pieces. Butter the bottom and sides of a 3½- or 4-quart crockery slow-cooker, and spread the batter in the bottom. Sprinkle with hazelnuts. Do not stir.

2. **Prepare second layer:** In a small bowl, combine sugar and cocoa. Sprinkle on top of first layer in the slow-cooker. Evenly drizzle on the hazelnut liqueur, if desired. Evenly pour the boiling water over the batter. Do not stir.

3. Cover and cook on HIGH for 2 to 2½ hours or until a tester inserted 1 inch deep into the center of the cake comes out clean.

4. To serve, spoon cake into individual serving dishes, spooning some of the pudding over the cake. Top with a dollop of whipped cream, a few chocolate curls, and a sprinkling of cinnamon, if desired.

Per serving: 533 calories, 7 g protein, 20 g total fat (4.2 g saturated), 83 g carbohydrates, 313 mg sodium, 15 mg cholesterol, 3 g dietary fiber

TO MAKE A SPICE BAG

It's easier to remove whole spices from a mixture when they're tied together in a spice bag. To make, cut a double thickness of cheesecloth into a 6- or 8-inch square. Place the whole spices in the center. Bring up the corners of the cheesecloth and tie with a piece of kitchen string.

ORANGE CREAM SAUCE

- 1 cup sugar
- ½ cup (1 stick) butter
- ½ cup heavy cream
- 1 tablespoon grated orange rind
- 1 tablespoon bourbon
  or 1 teaspoon vanilla extract

In a medium saucepan, combine sugar, butter, and cream. Cook over medium heat, stirring constantly, until mixture comes to a boil. Reduce heat and cook, uncovered, stirring constantly, for 5 minutes, until mixture thickens. Remove from heat and stir in orange rind and bourbon.

STEAMED CRANBERRY PUDDING

MAKES 8 SERVINGS

This recipe was given to me many years ago by my sister-in-law Helen, who was born and raised in Newton, Kansas. The pudding steams splendidly in a crockery slow-cooker and makes a nice change from plum pudding for the holidays. Since it's not overly sweet, it needs the sauce served alongside.

This recipe does not work well on LOW.

½ cup molasses
2 teaspoons baking soda
½ cup boiling water
1½ cups unbleached all-purpose flour

1 teaspoon baking powder
¾ teaspoon salt
1 1-pound package fresh cranberries, washed and picked over

1. Butter a 6- or 8-cup heat-proof mold that will fit into your 3½-quart or larger crockery slow-cooker. Place a metal rack or trivet in the slow-cooker.

2. In a large mixing bowl, combine molasses and baking soda. Pour in the boiling water. Stir in 1 cup of the flour, the baking powder, and salt.

3. Toss cranberries with the remaining ½ cup flour and stir them into molasses-flour mixture. Spoon batter into prepared mold. Cover with aluminum foil.

4. Place filled mold in center of rack. Pour in additional boiling water until it comes halfway up the sides of the mold. Cover and steam on HIGH for 3 to 4 hours, until a knife inserted near the center of the pudding comes out clean.

5. Just before serving, prepare Orange Cream Sauce, (see page 140).

6. To serve, loosen pudding by inserting a knife between pudding and sides of mold. Invert onto a platter. Serve warm with hot sauce.

**PREP TIME:
20 MIN**

**COOK TIME:
3-4 HR ON HIGH +
10 MIN ON STOVE
FOR MAKING
SAUCE**

Per serving: 420 calories, 3 g protein, 17 g total fat (10.6 g saturated), 65 g carbohydrates, 707 mg sodium, 51 mg cholesterol, 3 g dietary fiber

SOURCES

AMERICAN SPOON FOODS
(dried cherries and morels)
1668 Clarion Ave.
P.O. Box 566
Petoskey, MI 49770-0566
(800) 222-5886

VENISON AMERICA
(venison)
P.O. Box 86
Rosemount, MN 55068
(612) 435-9109

EICHTEN'S HIDDEN ACRES
(buffalo meat)
16705-310th Street
Center City, MN 55012
(612) 257-4752

FOREST RESOURCE CENTER
(shiitake mushrooms)
Route 2, Box 156A
Lanesboro, MN 55949
(507) 467-2437

MAYTAG DAIRY FARMS
(Maytag Blue Cheese)
P.O. Box 806
Newton, IA 50208
(800) 247-2458

WILD GAME, INC.
(pheasant and duck breasts)
2315 West Huron Street
Chicago, IL 60612
(312) 278-1661

INDEX